Endorsement of The Last Day of Winter
A Medical Perspective

The trust given to the authors by their patients have allowed them to reach into the depths of the taboo subject called death. Their patients have been the teachers for this thorough, thoughtful and explicit work which utilizes a seasonal metaphor to describe the various stages of the dying process. The "seasons of death" as a metaphor for dying richly flavors the text with the human side of the dying process. The book begins in the metaphorical September with feelings of apprehension as the disease process begins and ends on the last day of Winter in the terminal phase of the "Death" march This book succinctly outlines the scenarios of the passage into the next life and the bonds formed between the patient, their families and the care providers. As hospice care providers are acutely aware, palliative care patients are often neglected at the time when they need the most support and care. The authors do a wonderful job putting the unspeakable into a readable text to assist the terminally ill and their families and to teach future and current palliative care workers.

This book is a must read for any palliative care provider in order to provide insight into the world of the dying patient.

Eileen Gillan, MD
Assistant Professor, Pediatrics
Division of Hematology/Oncology
University of Connecticut Medical School

The Last Day of Winter

The Last Day of Winter

✦

Secrets from the Seasons of Dying

Jerry Griffin, MD, PharmD
and Pam Umann, MSW

iUniverse, Inc.
New York Lincoln Shanghai

The Last Day of Winter
Secrets from the Seasons of Dying

iUniverse books may be ordered through booksellers or by contacting:

iUniverse
2021 Pine Lake Road, Suite 100
Lincoln, NE 68512
www.iuniverse.com
1-800-Authors (1-800-288-4677)

ISBN-13: 978-0-595-34426-0 (pbk)
ISBN-13: 978-0-595-79186-6 (ebk)
ISBN-10: 0-595-34426-7 (pbk)
ISBN-10: 0-595-79186-7 (ebk)

Printed in the United States of America

Grief

Don't talk to me of grief

I have seen the red-rimmed eyes
of a sister
who spent all night
talking to her brother
dying of leukemia.

I have touched
the sagging shoulders
of a father
who stood twelve hours praying for his child
lying in a coma.

I have looked
at the lost, lonely face
in the mirror
shaving while you
return to the dust
of your origins.

I know there is
salve for wounds,
comfort for loss,
hope for reunion.
But let's not talk about that now.

—*Patrick W. Flanigan, MD*
"Surviving the Storm"

Contents

About the Authors. xiii

Introduction xv

CHAPTER 1 1
Spring and Summer
Seedlings and Synchronicity

CHAPTER 2 14
September
Season of Harvest

CHAPTER 3 35
October and November
First Frost

CHAPTER 4 73
Thanksgiving
Acknowledging the Bounty

CHAPTER 5 86
December
Winter Lights

CHAPTER 6 110
January and February
A Time to Die

CHAPTER 7 125
March 19th
The Last Day of Winter

CHAPTER 8.. 137
    Death of a Child
    When Children Lose a Parent

CHAPTER 9 153
    Post Season Concerns
    Grief

Epilogue 163

Epilogue 173

Index.. 177

Acknowledgments

We are immensely grateful to a host of talented and dedicated professionals in terminal and palliative care, as well as those in writing and publications.

First and foremost, however, we are grateful to our patients. They have been our teachers. They have invited us into their most intimate moments and have allowed us to share their experiences with you.

We are indebted to our editor, Leigh Fortson, who not only gave unselfishly of herself but also became our friend.

We are grateful Barbara Neighbors Deal, PhD, for her expert guidance and faith in us and in our work.

The support we both received from our colleagues is remarkable. In Pam's case, the encouragement she received from her friends and associates at Saint Louise Regional Hospital was invaluable. She is particularly grateful for the unwavering encouragement of her friends, Sister Camille Cuadra, Sister Mary Peter Diaz, and Sister Paula Baker. Their enthusiasm for this work and their unflagging optimism got her through the hard times. For Jerry, the encouragement and support by the hospice team of the Central Coast Visiting Nurse Association and Hospice were invaluable.

We thank our colleagues in the Salinas, Monterey, Silicon Valley, and Gilroy, California, medical communities, many of whom reviewed chapters of this book when it was in its infancy. We are especially grateful to Dr. Patrick Flanigan, whose poetry appears throughout this book. The support Jerry received from the medical professionals he encountered in the US Army was also very valuable. Colonels Sara Ferril and Kathy Lenihan gave unbiased and valuable advice.

We appreciate Ira Byock, MD, for his encouragement and help in the early stages of writing this book…

Lastly, we are immensely thankful to our families. To Jerry's wife, Carolyn, and his daughters, Sarah, Renate, and Katie; to Pam's daughter, Sheila, her step-daughter, Tianna, her stepson, Anthony, and to her grandchildren, Zack, Corbin, and Rayna: thank you and bless you for your unfailing love, patience, and understanding. This is your story, too.

About the Authors

Jerry Griffin

Gerald Dieter Griffin grew up in Germany during the post-war years and came to the United States as the adopted son of an American army sergeant. As an "army brat," Jerry moved around the country and back to Germany several times, before settling in San Francisco. During college, he met and married Carolyn King. Jerry has doctoral degrees in both medicine and pharmacy. After starting life as an academic (assistant professor of clinical pharmacy/pharmacology at the University of New Mexico in Albuquerque), he earned his medical degree. By the time he finished his residency in emergency medicine, he was forty-two and his three daughters were in high school. He left active duty in 1985 and has served in the Army Reserve on and off active duty since that time.

In his spare time, Jerry practiced emergency medicine, general internal medicine, and pharmacology. He was the medical director of Hospice of the Central Coast from 1989 to 1997. Early in 1997 Jerry became medical director of the Visiting Nurse Association and Hospice of Monterey County.

Jerry was called up by the Army to participate in Desert Storm and Operation Provide Comfort I. He retired as the commanding general of a medical brigade, and he still considers himself a soldier. Jerry was "unretired" to serve again in the global war on terror and completed a year in Iraq.

Pam Umann

Pam Umann spent her childhood in New Orleans and relocated to the San Francisco Bay Area as a high school student in 1966. The political and social climate of San Francisco in the mid 1960s to 1970s impacted her in ways that continue to emerge today.

Pam has a master's degree in social welfare from the University of California at Berkeley. She has worked with hospitals, hospice agencies and home-care services since 1990. She has provided crisis intervention in emergency rooms and in intensive-care units and has facilitated bereavement support programs throughout the San Francisco Bay Area. Pam has developed a specialization in life-threatening illness—particularly AIDS and cancer.

Pam maintains an active interest in complementary healing practices and has studied hypnotherapy and Reiki. She is a certified hypnotherapist and a level II Reiki practitioner.

Her work in the medical field is supplemented by her interest in spirituality and how spirit manifests in our lives and in our deaths. Pam has developed and facilitated workshops, trainings, and weekend retreats in the San Francisco area and in Calistoga and Monterey.

Pam has a daughter, a stepdaughter, and a stepson, as well as three grandchildren. They are her heroes.

Surviving the Storm

How do they do it?

How do dolphins and great whales

survive through nightlong storms

when white capped waves

cover the ocean from horizon to horizon

when spray fills the air

and rain falls down in solid sheets?

How do they suck air

into their huge lungs without drowning

in the water all around them?

They must know the secrets that we know.

They must know the secrets that help us

smile and breathe and survive

without drowning in the sorrow all around us.

They must be able to

see the beauty of a raindrop,

hear the song of the wind,

feel their belonging to the Universe.

—*Patrick Flanigan, MD*

Seasonal Metaphors

We begin with the metaphorical September. You begin to sense that something is wrong. There are vague, troublesome "stirrings" and feelings of apprehension. From the beginning, we go with you through the progressive and inexorable steps by which one loosens the hold on life and ultimately dies.

The metaphorical October and November is the time of diagnosis and increasing turmoil. Disease progression brings physical changes and loss of function in the body. This is the time when decisions have to be made. This is the time when the soul-searching begins, and dying still seems far away. Perhaps there is still some hope for survival.

Thanksgiving comes at the end of October and November and is the turning point towards acceptance. It is time to reap the harvest of a life well lived and to stop plowing the fields of life.

The metaphorical December is the "festival of lights," and it becomes the time of soul-searching and reflection resulting in greater acceptance and appreciation of life as it was lived. Everyone who cares for your dying loved one can participate in the process of life review. December is a time of insights and epiphanies. The true gifts of our time together are opened, appreciated, and shared.

January and February bring accelerated physical and emotional symptoms of dying. This is often accompanied by deep depression. This is a pivotal and crucially important time in the dying process. It may also well be the most difficult for all of you.

The "death march" ends on the 19th of March, the last day of winter. There will be physical and emotional challenges. There will be pain and fear. We will explore all of it. Dying is the process of *coming in*: of reflection, of coming to terms with the life that you have lived. Dying is learning to warm yourself on the hearth of your own soul. It is not a time to plant. It is not a time to reap.

Death is a time when the deeds of your life have sprouted like seeds planted in a long-ago spring, and these deeds have brought you past the time of harvest. The seeds you planted deepest in the richest soil—your hopes for eternity—lie fallow in the earth, and you crawl slowly into the cave of your soul and wait for the transformation that our religions and our traditions and the wisdom of our own hearts tell us will surely follow. Magic and transformation happen in the dark places: in the caves, in the sadness, in the solitude.

Death is the winter of the soul. It is when gargoyles stand watch and old women dance in the moonlight to welcome the season of the *going in*. It is the time when the holy men of Tibet seek shelter from the mountain storms and do their sacred rituals in secret places. It is the season of dying.

The man just came by

To close up summer for the winter

He turned off the Ferris wheel

Took down the moon

Put You in his truck

And drove away

Muffler splattering ice on the dusty road

We walked yesterday

—*Carrie Hyde, poet*

1

SPRING AND SUMMER
SEEDLINGS AND SYNCHRONICITY

For Pam, the seeds of this book were planted in the springtime of her life. She was a young mother, barely into her twenties, when she was told that her father had an incurable cancer.

The Night My Father Died: Pam's Epiphany

My father was a merchant-marine captain during and after World War II. He was gone a lot of the time, and he was alone most of his life. But he was the quintessential officer: a ship's captain. His whole life evolved around the fact that he was the captain. This was his personage, his existence, and the source of his strength and also his weakness.

My father died alone in a small room at the end of a hall. The whole family was home that night. My mother was asleep in the room next door. I was at the kitchen table playing Monopoly with my husband and my aunt. No one was with my father as he took his last breath. No one knew if he was frightened or in pain, or if he struggled or went gently. It was not from lack of love that my father met his death in heart-numbing isolation. It was simply the culmination of escalating fear and careening ignorance.

My mother had called me months before. "Your father has cancer," she said. After many months of increasingly unusual behavior, my father was diagnosed with a large brain tumor. Surgery was performed that afternoon.

The doctors explained that my father's brain tumor was not a primary cancer, but rather a metastasis from his lungs. The cancer was widespread throughout his body by the time it was discovered. My mother turned to my brother and me and said very simply, "We will not discuss this with your father. We will not say the word *cancer* in his presence. We will go on as if nothing has happened."

And so we went on as if nothing had happened. Except, of course, for the changes. My father went to daily radiation treatment. We all managed to abstain from ever using the word *cancer* in my father's presence, and my father accommodated us by never using the word *cancer* in our presence. And so the word was effectively eliminated from our world—except for the large sign above the door of the cancer center where he went for his daily treatments.

It is impossible to block one word from your vocabulary. Words carry meanings and concepts, and it was the meaning of my father's illness that we were all colluding to deny. The absence of speaking is silence. And for every word unsaid and every thought unspoken, huge gray slabs of silence were laid between us like the stones in Frost's "Mending Wall."

Before I built a wall I'd ask to know

What I was walling out or walling in

And to whom I was like to give offense.

…Something there is that doesn't love a wall

…That wants it down.

—*Robert Frost*

Spring came, and my father planted roses on the side of the house. He spent long afternoons resting on the couch with my infant daughter cuddled against him. I don't know what his thoughts were as he whispered into her tiny ears. I don't know what he wanted me to know or if there was something special he wanted me to remember about him. I don't know if he was in pain. The silence had won. We were strangers to each other.

My father died on a chilly November night. My mother called me and told to come and bring clothes to stay overnight. She did not say why, and I did not ask. My father was lying in a hospital bed that Mom had brought to the house. He was in the last bedroom at the end of the hall. He could not see out the window from the bed. He could not see the roses he had planted. He could see little more than the ceiling and the walls. I'm not sure what he saw that day. His eyes were flashing about, unfocused. He was shaking terribly. He could not talk. I sat at his bedside for a few minutes, holding his hand and trying to find words to say. My mother became very upset and insisted that we leave the room. "Your father needs his rest." Even then, I knew it was a peculiar thing to say. I checked on my father from time to time throughout the afternoon and evening, but I never stayed long at his bedside. If I remained with him for more than a few minutes, my mother would come for me. "Your father needs his rest."

At about eleven o'clock, I lost the Monopoly game and went to check on Dad. I remember pausing and listening for his breathing. I didn't hear him breathing...or did I? I paused three or four times before I found myself standing in the doorway to his room. His chest didn't seem to be moving, and I still couldn't hear his breathing. I walked very slowly into the room, watching and listening for any sounds of life.

There were none. The silence we had placed between us was thundering. Even the walls were throbbing.

In this book, there are many stories of triumph over fear and isolation: stories of people who pass peacefully in the arms of loved ones; stories of people who share their journeys and who find meaning and resolution at life's end. But for me, the real impetus for this book came from the death of a man who was not able to do any of these things, who was not allowed to voice his sorrow, his pain, or his fear to any of us—a man who walked his path in stony silence and who died alone in a small room at the end of the hall. More than anything else, this is my apology to him.

Jerry had visited the Gila Wilderness as a child, but its lessons were given to him in the summer of his life, after he had learned to reflect and to draw wisdom from his experience.

The Bridge in the Gila Wilderness: Jerry's Epiphany

In the fall of 1990, I vacationed in the Gila Wilderness of New Mexico. I had been there as a Boy Scout, and I had fond memories of a beautiful forest where people are friendly, honest, and trustworthy. I felt at home and safe there.

Just from being there, I felt my sense of humor returning and my emotional well-being renewing itself. The Gila River was only fifty feet away—great to swim in, great to skip rocks on, and great to sit by and listen to the water. It was a time of healing.

Among the special and sacred places of the Gila are the cliff dwellings. The Mogollon people who lived there so long ago disappeared without a trace. The caves they lived in are carved out of solid rock: some carved by nature and time, and some by Mogollon hands. The caves are hidden in the cliffs of a deep canyon. The terrain is difficult, and the park rangers are vigilant in protecting the dwellings from casual tourists. Few people know they are even there.

I remembered them from my years of scouting in the area and felt attracted to this site of wonder and mystery. I knew instinctively that this was part of my renewal.

I started up the canyon and recognized the stations I knew well. The climb was steep, and progress was slow. Finally, I was there. The sun was starting to set over the other side of the canyon, but I estimated that I would have at least one hour of daylight. I quickly climbed up the ladder to the largest chamber and onto a loft, from where I could see the whole village. I sat there for a long time in the quiet, trying to imagine how life in this village was before the Mogollon people left. It must have been teeming with activity—a whole community of several hundred, living around this large room and using it as a center of community life.

When the Mogollon people disappeared, they left fires and ashes, corn (or maize), and kitchen utensils in place. They left the things of everyday living. It is almost as if they expected to come back some day.

Suddenly, I became aware of voices around me. They were soft at first, then became louder. People were talking: children laughing, a baby crying, men and women talking. The village below me was alive again, and vibrant. I saw people who seemed to know I was there, but were neither frightened nor concerned. They seemed to be pointing to me and trying to get my attention; they were also pointing to the other side of the canyon, which was about one hundred yards away, and just as high as the side with the dwellings.

On the other side of the canyon I saw campfires and more people. Although I could not see their feet or their legs, they seemed to be moving around at a fast pace. I could not hear them, but they were there. As I glanced back to this side of the canyon, I saw a bridge made up of two logs over which people were walking slowly to the other side. Once they reached the other side, they became livelier and more animated and joined the rest of the people there in their happy activities. They did not look back or show any concern for the villagers on this side.

At this point, I saw the sun starting to go down behind the opposite side of the canyon's rim, and all of a sudden, I was alone. The people, the voices, the laughter, and the talking were gone. I got scared, feeling all the more alone. I do not remember how I got off that loft, down the pole, and down the canyon to the ranger station.

I believe that the Mogollon people were showing me what had happened to them. They had learned how to cross the log bridge between life and death. They crossed over effortlessly, happily, and without fear. The log bridge was the link between both worlds. Flanked by the enduring mountains, you could see that both the village and the other side were part of a larger landscape. In the same way, the Mogollon people knew that both life and death are part of a larger existence.

We join spokes

together in a wheel

but it is the center hole

that makes the wagon move

—*Tao Te Ching*

Synchronicity: A Primer

The springtime of life, when the world is new and fresh, is the time of epiphanies and sudden knowing. Sometimes it takes a while to know what we have learned. The knowledge has to sit awhile. It has to season in the warmth of life as it is lived. Sometimes it isn't until the summer of life that we begin to notice patterns and coincidences. And sometimes we notice the imprint of something that cannot be explained away as simple coincidence. And so, sometime in the summer, we learn about synchronicity.

Nature, a reflection of our soul,

Reveals the seasons of our lives.

Like people, earth's seasons teach us

Patience, awareness, and encourage us to grow.

From the sparkle of sunlight in the doe's eye

To the sparrow elevated by the air below it's wings

The spirit of God is this source of life that fuels our spirit

And raises us above pain and sorrow.

Only the soul can travel to this place above the clouds

Where we are lifted by the breath of God.

Here, the lessons learned in nature

Disclose to us that dying is a transition into life

And nothing completely disappears.

Rather, we are transformed into another realm of existence

To experience the essence of life

Where the soul never dies.

—*Sam Oliver*
   "What the Dying Teach Us"
   1998, Haworth Press, Inc. NY

Psychiatrist Carl Jung defines synchronicity as the concept that links two separately occurring, seemingly random events together in such a way that a shared meaning is imparted to both events. These connected events may not be easily explainable by the simplistic cause-and-effect relationships we look for in Western medicine and health care. Synchronicity is the element found in *coincidental or random* events that transforms the meaning of the event and imparts connection where there was once only randomness.

Jung describes three basic types of synchronicity, as follows:

1. A coincidence between a mental process—a thought or a feeling—and an external event. These may be separated by a minute, a decade, or a lifetime. An example of this would be if someone were to say, "I could sure use a bite to eat." Moments later, a pizza-delivery boy rings the doorbell and cannot find the house that allegedly ordered the food. He makes a call, finds out the order was a prank, and happily gives it to the person who just voiced his desire for something to eat. It seems almost as if telepathy has played a role.

2. Someone has a dream or vision that coincides with an event that is actually happening or has actually taken place, perhaps far away, and is verified at a later date.

3. Someone has a dream, vision, or premonition that something will happen in the future. This type of synchronicity appears to be the most common.

Here's a classic example of synchronicity: A woman we know was recuperating from surgery and had been on state disability for several months. Her savings were almost gone. She was having coffee with a friend and said, "My last disability payment is June 15. If I am not working by July, I don't know what I'll do."

Just then the phone rang. On the other end was a friend with whom she hadn't spoken in years. "Am I calling you at home or at work?" he asked.

"My home," she replied, "I don't have a work number." Without missing a beat, he answered, "Would you like to have a work number? I have a job opportunity for you."

The meaning in these two obviously connected events was not in the coffee conversation, nor did it come from the telephone call. Rather, it came from the synthesis of the two events.

How *exactly* does this happen and what drives it? That is one of the mysteries of the universe. A wise man once told me: *The questions are more interesting than the answers.* And so it is with synchronicity. We don't know exactly how it works. We do know what it *does*.

Synchronistic events affirm our connection to each other and the world and reveal that there is no ultimate isolation or separation.

Jimmy's Owl

I was sitting with Joann in her living room, drinking lemon tea and looking at childhood photographs of her son, Jimmy. Jimmy had died the preceding summer in an automobile accident in the Denali Wilderness in Alaska. He had been twenty-one years old and off on his big Alaskan adventure. Joann closed the book, poured another cup of tea, and asked if I had time to listen to her story of the incidents that preceded Jimmy's death.

Jimmy had a black Labrador retriever who had been his constant companion since early childhood. The boy and the dog had been inseparable. As Jimmy grew into his youth, the dog grew old. When Jimmy set off for college, it was clear that the dog's days were coming to an end. Joann watched the dog become more feeble and crippled and tried to nurse him along at least until Jimmy could come home for summer vacation. But it was not to be. When she took the dog into the vet one spring day, he told her that the dog had cancer and was in great pain. Very reluctantly, she agreed to have the dog put to sleep. That night, she called Jimmy to tell him what had happened, dreading his response. But he was very calm and very accepting of the situation.

"It's okay, Mom," he had assured her, "you did the right thing. I'm all right. Really, I am."

They spoke quietly for some time about the dog, and then Jimmy announced his plans for the summer: he and his childhood friend, Art, were going to drive to Alaska and backpack into the Denali Wilderness as the base of Mt. McKinley. Joann was immediately filled with a sense of foreboding and begged Jimmy not to go—or at least not to drive.

"Can't you fly there?" she asked him. Jimmy would have none of her concern. He was determined, and he was excited about this great adventure.

A few days before departing from college, Jimmy called Joann again. He excitedly went over his plans with her, assuring her that her concerns were ungrounded. Then, as he was saying goodbye, Jimmy asked Joann, "Do you know how much I love you?"

Joann said that she did and was about to hang up the phone when Jimmy stopped her. "No," he insisted, "sit down. Listen to me. I want to tell you how much I love you."

Joann sat and listened while her youngest son recounted to her the things she had done for him in his life, the special times they had shared, and the qualities in her that he most cherished and admired. "And now," he said, "you know how much I love you."

Jimmy and Art set out for Alaska the next day in Art's old Bronco. They camped along the way, finally making it to Anchorage, where they stayed for a week before setting out for Denali.

During this time, Joann decided to go to her summer home in Tahoe, hoping a change of scenery would mitigate her growing sense of foreboding. The Tahoe house was a warm, happy place filled with memorabilia from her family's younger years. Her first day there was peaceful and serene. That night, Joann was awakened by a strange moaning sound, like that of a wounded animal. She was familiar with the night sounds and the animals that lived in the woods surrounding the house. This was something she had never heard before. It seemed to come from quite near the house—just outside her windows. The sound persisted on and off throughout the night.

In the morning, Joann was concerned enough to call her eldest son and ask him to drive up to Tahoe to join her. Bud got to the house that afternoon.

The second evening, the moaning sound happened again, and again, it was quite near the house. Bud took a flashlight and went outside on the deck to see if he could identify where the sound was coming from. Joann was in the kitchen when she heard Bud call to her, "Mom, come out here. You've got to see this."

Joann joined Bud on the deck as he pointed the flashlight to a tree near the house. In the fork of the tree sat an enormous silver owl. In the twenty years she had owned this cabin, she had never seen an owl. Suddenly, the owl flew off the tree and swooped down onto the railing of the deck, very near to Joann and Bud. It sat there for a few minutes, looking at them, then flew into the forest.

The next morning the police came to the door to tell Joann of Jimmy's death two nights earlier in Denali—the first night at Tahoe.

"If it hadn't been for the owl," she said, "I wouldn't have called Bud. I would have been alone when they came to tell me." The owl had come the night of Jimmy's death.

Several months later, Joann finally summoned the courage to go through some of Jimmy's things in the basement of her California home. She had always saved samples of her children's creative work as they were growing up. Jimmy was the artist. As she was going through his old schoolwork, Joann came across some art she had saved from eighth grade—ten years before his death. There were two large pictures: a landscape with a mountain in the background and a large decoupage painting of a silver owl. His picture is framed now and is on her living room wall. There is no doubt that it is the same owl that visited her the night of Jimmy's death.

Jimmy's friend, Art, survived the accident. Following many months of recupera-
tion, he was visiting Joann before returning to college when he saw the picture of
the owl in her living room. Joann told Art the story of the owl at Tahoe and how
she had found this owl from the eighth grade, along with a landscape he had
done in pastels. Art had been in Jimmy's eighth grade class and remembered
many of their art projects, although he didn't remember the owl. He asked to see
the landscape. Art's face went white when she presented it to him. "That's where
we were, Joann," he said. "That's the road. Look, there's Mt. McKinley in the
background."

Synchronistic magic is a catalyst that can happen at any time in life and dying. It
is out of time and out of sequence. It turns us, spins us, and, ultimately, propels
us into another direction entirely. Death is synchronistic. It connects several
seemingly "unrelated" things. The death of your loved one happens in a social
context. It is connected to every event, past, present, and future, in your life. And
death is also cataclysmic. It changes everything in the blink of an eye. Noticing
the synchronistic events that surround you may help you make sense of it all. It
may give you a moment to catch your breath and appreciate the sacred and the
magical as it unfolds in the midst of all of your sadness.

You, sent out beyond your recall,

Go to the limits of your longing.

Embody me.

Flare up life a flame

And make big shadows I can move in.

Let everything happen to you: Beauty and terror

Just keep going. No feeling is final.

Don't let yourself lose me.

Nearby is the country they call life.

You will know it by its seriousness.

Give me your hand

—*Rainer Maria Rilke*

2

SEPTEMBER: THE SEASON OF HARVEST

To everything there is a season

And a time for every purpose under heaven.

—*Ecclesiastes*

The Falling Leaves: Early Fears and Suspicions

The seasons of dying begin with September. The sun, still warm on the fields, begins to dim. We notice shadows where there was light. We go searching for afghans and sweaters to ward off the coolness of the season. There is a chill in the air. Even as we are tending to the last flowers of summer, our minds are aware of the approaching fall and winter. With every leaf that falls, we are reminded that a season of darkness is approaching. This chapter is about the beginning of the dying process—early autumn in the progression from life to death—and how life is changing for you and your loved one.

This is the time when your loved one starts paying attention to things he ignored up to now. This is when he decides to go to the doctor about what's ailing him: that persistent pain, a small amount of blood in the stool, a bothersome twitch, inexplicable tiredness and malaise, exhaustion, insomnia, a tremor, unusual pressure in his head, occasional dizziness, or blurred vision. There may be a single symptom, or there be many, but there is a definite underlying feeling of wariness and apprehension. You are also aware that all may not be well with your loved one. This is the beginning of the dying process. It is early autumn.

Carol

Carol had always taken excellent care of her health. She was careful about her diet, got a lot of fresh air and exercise, and meditated every day. She had been post-menopausal for five years when she became aware of mild cramping and a persistent bloated feeling. Her abdomen became swollen and hard. Carol thought at first that she was developing constipation from her iron supplement. She stopped taking the supplement. She tried herbal teas from the health-food store. She eliminated certain foods from her diet. It wasn't until she noticed intermittent vaginal bleeding that Carol finally went to see her gynecologist. The doctor diagnosed uterine cancer that had spread beyond her pelvis.

Carol's first reaction was shock and disbelief. Upon reflection, she realized that she had lived with the cancer for some time, and, that at some level of her soul, she had known of its presence in her life.

Receiving the Diagnosis

I went

to Break the News to Her

and I could hear my own heart beat

With dread of what my own lips would say.

—*W.W. Gibson*

It seemed simple enough: your loved one went to the doctor to discuss the symptoms that had been bothersome for a while. The doctor listened and followed through with a physical examination. Some laboratory tests were taken. Blood was drawn, a urine sample was taken, an x-ray or a CT scan was performed. There may have been a biopsy to see if a growth was abnormal. The doctor may have checked his lymph nodes to determine if any disease or infection has spread from the original site.

(The lymph system is a system of channels that parallels the arteries and veins all over the body. It is where the body puts its refuse—the poisons and toxins from infection, old or dead blood cells, used chemicals, and sometimes, cancer cells. The infection and toxins are then routed through this system and gotten rid of by the body. When there is infection or disease that is spreading or being thrown away via the lymph system, then the doctor can feel the little bumps we all call nodes. That means that there is something in those "trash collection centers" in the lymph system.)

Then, there were the days of waiting for the test results. (Lab results usually arrive in three to ten days—difficult days. If the samples are sent out to a special lab, it can take longer. Just three days can seem like forever.) Then the doctor received the lab results. The news was not good.

Getting a diagnosis of a life-threatening illness is always a shock—to everyone, even to the doctor. It doesn't matter if it was preceded by scores of medical tests, deep apprehension over time, and a warning from the doctor that the results could be grave. Nothing can adequately prepare your loved one, or those who occupy his or her life, for the words "terminal illness."

The doctor discussed the results with you, explained what they meant, and gave you some sense of what to anticipate in the days ahead. As the doctor presented the findings, you and your loved one likely experienced an intense sense of urgency. You and your loved one didn't really focus on the lab results; all you saw was the potential end of his life, and pain, arriving as a set of data on paper.

After the results were thoroughly explained, you and your loved one began to discuss treatment options with the doctor. At that time—and at every interaction with the doctor in the future—you should have been treated with honesty and compassion. After receiving the terminal diagnosis, you may have been in shock and unable to effectively discuss treatment. If you think that may have happened, make another appointment with the doctor to explore treatment options again. Be sure to include your loved one in these office visits.

Medicine defines diagnosis as the act or process of identifying or determining the nature and cause of a disease or injury through evaluation of patient history, examination, and review of laboratory data. This definition speaks to a medical mind. It does not cover the emotional questions or issues experienced by you or your loved as you received the diagnosis. Diagnosis, in your loved one's mind, could likely be interpreted as "Why me?" or "This isn't really happening." He will probably sort through it many times by searching back to the very first symptoms that occurred.

After the Diagnosis

Life is changing. The news of a terminal illness is a watershed event. The way your loved one perceives his life, the decisions he makes, the priorities he establishes, and the memories he treasures will all undergo radical transformations. Life will never be the same again for him or those who love him.

As strength wanes and emotions fluctuate, the patterns you have learned to call normal also shift. Shock, trauma, and physical debilitation from the terminal illness will impact every aspect of your loved one's life. Expect fluctuations in his personality. One minute he will be bouncing around the house, chatting nervously about everything except his illness. The next minute he will be glued to the computer, researching everything on the Internet that pertains to a medication. Ten minutes later he will be staring blankly into the future. He will be silent and brooding.

His attention to normal activities may also become erratic. One week he will go to the gym every day and eat only organically grown vegetables. The next week he'll stay in his pajamas for three days straight and you will catch him smoking on the back porch. He hasn't smoked for twenty years. "What's the difference?" he asks, shrugging, "I'm going to die anyway."

Layers of shock and grief take up space in the brain. There will be forgetfulness, and he may have trouble concentrating. He could become indecisive. His feelings of competence diminish, and he could feel very needy.

Things around the house and in your environment will change, too. Laundry won't get done. He may skip some meals, and cancel appointments—or not show up at all. Some days he may stay in bed all day watching infomercials on television.

Some of these changes are transitory. Others will wax and wane until the end.

If your loved one was the manager of the household, someone will have to provide assistance. The children still need to get to school. The family still needs to eat, and laundry must be done. Bills need to be paid. The lawn still needs to be mowed. The dog still needs to be walked. Food still has to be bought and then cooked. Whatever roles your loved one was used to performing will have to be delegated elsewhere. But they still need to be done. At some point, you will need to get help.

If money is not an issue, hire someone to do the household maintenance so you can concentrate on the changes in your life. If you don't have a lot of money, you may need to enlist family and friends to keep the wheels spinning. Learn how to delegate. Often, church communities provide this kind of help. Talk with your minister, priest or rabbi. In some states, Medicaid insurance programs include a benefit called In-Home Supportive Services (IHSS). A housekeeper comes to the home for a predetermined number of hours each week. This person provides personal care, assistance with household chores, shopping, cooking, and running errands.

How Your Life Will Change as a Caregiver

Your loved one's declining health and eventual death will bring about many changes in your own life. Some of the changes will occur gradually, while others may happen quite suddenly. For example:

- You will have less time to participate in your usual activities.

- You may have to make changes in the very basic aspects of your life. Perhaps you will need to move from your home in the suburbs to care for a parent in another city.

- People who once slept snugly in the same bed may no longer be able to share a bedroom. Medical equipment and physical incapacity may make you feel shut out of your loved one's life.

- Relationships also change. Disease and treatment can cause physical changes and disfigurement. Your loved one may no longer feel comfortable with the easy intimacy you once enjoyed. He may no longer undress in your presence. He may also withdraw emotionally as he struggles to cope with unwanted changes.

- Your role and your responsibilities to your loved one will become complex. You are no longer simply the partner, sibling, lover, or child. You are now also the caregiver and, in some cases, the decision-maker. Both of you may feel uncomfortable with this change, and there may be resentment.

Contemplating Death and Surviving Chaos

With your loved one's diagnosis, daily habits change, and so do daily thoughts. Your loved one is facing his mortality, and, as part of this process, so are you. This is a time when you will think about death a great deal and probably ask questions that are difficult or impossible to answer. One commonly asked question is "What will death be like?"

Death is as individual as life. Everyone's experiences will be different. Some people have years to live with a terminal illness. Others will survive only six months, or even six weeks. No matter what the circumstances or issues of the death of the person for whom you are a caregiver, our objective is to guide you so that you may help your mother, father, sister, brother, friend, colleague, grandparent, relative, child, other loved one, or yourself as the last days of life are apparent. We want to be a part of the first link in the chain of support to help you and your loved one. This is not only about the losses and miracles your loved one will experience. It is also about your losses and miracles. And they will be many, they will be great, and they will be demanding.

We write about death in a linear way, as if that's the way it occurs. It does not. Death, like life, sometimes feels like it happens randomly, with no connection to the world—with no intrinsic value or meaning. Life and death are not random. They both occur in a context. They are interwoven. Death and life coexist in each discrete moment in time. And it doesn't happen in a linear pattern. In real life, it all happens at once, instantaneously and continuously.

A woman who was being treated for cancer wrote about it this way:

> *The world is acting upon me and I am dancing as fast as I can and there are mind explosions and heart explosions and soul explosions and my body is betraying me and my friends are betraying me and my Social Security hasn't come and I had a dream about my mother and my hair is falling out and I thought I heard God talking to me yesterday but it was the dentist and who am I really and where is my Social Security check and this is really scary and I'm not going to any damn support groups and why am I so sleepy and why am I so confused and gee everything's clearer now and oh my God I'm bald and will I survive this and...*

You may have already noticed a similar chaos in your loved one as he attempts to make sense of the unfathomable. This is normal. It is part of the process of absorbing the shock of the situation. Be patient and attentive. Listen to the anger and confusion, but don't try to impart order. Simply listen. Nod. Reassure your loved one that you are in it for the long haul and will stick by him through all the ups and downs. Then, continue listening. As your loved one attempts to put together the pieces of what has shattered, he will do much of it out loud. This is the external experience taking hold. It feels to your loved one as though some invisible force has taken him by the scruff of the neck and is wildly shaking him, like a rag doll, continuing to shatter every last brittle sense of what was once real and unshakable.

As he goes through the shock and trauma of accepting his mortality, one of the most valuable gifts you can give him is simply to be a good listener.

Most of us are familiar with the story of the woman who went to dinner with her new boyfriend. She had laryngitis and could barely speak. She spent the evening nodding politely and expressing surprise with her facial expressions. She listened without comment. At the end of the evening, the man ran into a friend who asked how the date had gone. "It was wonderful," he replied. "She is the most brilliant and articulate woman I have ever met."

People need to be heard and understood. They need to be able to tell their stories their way and to have their versions of their own lives validated and respected. In its highest form, listening is nothing less than bearing witness to your loved one's very existence. Here's how to become the kind of listener that will help your loved one feel comfortable:

- Make eye contact intermittently. You want your loved one to feel connected and heard, not examined. Move your gaze once in a while to his shoulder or to another spot in the room. Then return to his eyes.

- If you are seated opposite each other, lean forward a little in your chair. A friendly, open body image conveys your support and acceptance of what he is saying.

- Make occasional body contact. Holding a hand or reaching out to touch a shoulder is an expression of affection and caring.

- Try not to use negative terms like, "Why didn't you go to the doctor sooner?" or, "I told you to stop smoking years ago." These are of no value now.

- Don't make judgmental comments, even if you think your loved one is being too dramatic, in denial, or just wrong about something.

- Use supportive comments like, "I can see how it would feel that way to you."

- Ask helpful questions. Do not ask, "Why do you feel that way?" Instead ask, "Can you tell me more about what that was like for you?"

From the Outside, In

For most people, death approaches quietly, sometimes almost imperceptibly. In the beginning, death seems to come from the outside, in. One moment, your loved one may be engaged in life—moving ever forward with dreams, frustrations, and aspirations. The next moment, he may be taking his final breath.

We once heard a hospice nurse speaking with the family of a dying man, explaining the physiological processes that occur in the last days and hours of life. She said to the family, "People die from the inside, out." This describes the final moment, when the body releases its last hold on life.

What she meant is that the experience of dying transcends from an external one to an internal one. In the course of a life-threatening illness, losses are cumulative, such that the process is first perceived as an experience happening outside oneself, or externally. Soon enough, however, it shifts inward. This seems like a paradox, but look at it this way: the psychological sense of death seems to come like an alien—from the outside—as an intruder, when in fact, the cause of your loved one's death comes from the inside—literally—of his body.

Somehow, these two opposites need to cross paths and meet each other. Ideally, this must happen without more chaos and fear. It is at this interface, or crossover where the external meets the internal (when death is acknowledged), that we as caregivers and family members can be most useful. Learn the subtle changes that occur as the experience goes from external to internal (from talkative/chaotic to quiet/meditative/calm). This phase can test your patience and stamina, and you can expect some difficulty—but this is normal. Holding steady for your loved one is the best way to keep him from being fearful himself and to ultimately help this transition. Once the crossover occurs successfully, your loved one will internalize both the internal and external experiences as one.

Perhaps this process is part of an innate sense of immortality. You finally release life from your body, lose the body, and become one with the external again—a true paradox, but an understandable one. Even when it emanates from the very cells of your body, death is alien to the eternal nature of your soul.

The Dream

One minute you're rolling through life like a Wells Fargo stagecoach—perhaps wobbling a little when you hit a rut in the road, but making ground nevertheless. Next thing you know, the bad guys have surrounded you, guns drawn, shooting at the sky. People are screaming. The air is foul with the smell of gunpowder and dark with swirling dust and smoke. You look to the horizon and you don't see the cavalry on the hill. "That's it, then," you think, "I'm a goner."

Symbols, Spirituality, and the Approach of Death

You wake up and reflect on the dream, then get out the dream interpretation book and look up all the symbols that showed up in the dream. Whatever their meaning, you realize that the symbols emanate from you. You are the source of both the symbols and their meaning. Although they manifest in the world, their origins are deep within your soul. The Native Americans understood this concept, as shown through a rough translation of one of their prayers:

Oh, Great Spirit

Earth, sun, sky and sea

You are inside

And all around me

—*Native American Prayer*
(interpreted by Wings of Song)

Your spiritual identity exists in the far reaches of the universe and in the most hidden and protected places in your heart. Your connection to your god and the world is actualized by your own innermost feelings and is reflected back to you in the external world. This is one of the best-kept secrets in the universe. It is written everywhere and taught by nearly every major religious tradition. Yet it is obscured from memory by attachment to the body. People often think, "I am my body."

When that happens, you forget who you are. Death, in peeling away the body, reminds you that you are not a physical being having a spiritual experience. You are really a spiritual being having a physical experience.

Although death is a natural process, those who have been given a finite period of time to live—and those who care for them—experience the process of death as awkward and utterly unnatural. Death, as it approaches, feels like an alien intruder. The truth is that your loved one may have been living with dying for quite a while. Even so, he has already begun to negotiate a relationship with his impending death. His body knows this. It has already made accommodations to internal changes you are only beginning to perceive as caregiver. His soul is also aware that the time for preparation has come. This dying—this change from being heartily engaged in life to taking a final breath—is a long and winding path full of pain, fear, and loneliness. But it can also be rich with adventure and discovery.

Early Caregiving Hints

Death is a contemplative time. As you and your loved one walk this path together, be mindful that you will probably spend time doing and thinking about things that are out of your ordinary routine. For example:

• Expect to undergo soul-searching so you can comfort, enlighten, and inspire your dying loved one.

- Read and learn about your loved one's illness and care.

- Allow yourself to begin the grieving process, and if you're comforted, read about it.

- Believe in yourself.

Losses Come Early

If I can keep this pain alive

the outrage will sustain the hope

and I'll survive.

But if I learn to softly sigh

at your indifference,

then I'll die

—*Carrie Hyde*

The changes and losses brought about by declining health include social and financial losses, as well as losses of family roles, and changes in relationships. Death is often perceived erroneously as a specific moment in time when the body's processes cease—the last heartbeat, the final breath. It's true that the end of life is a dramatic and defining passage, but it usually doesn't happen in a matter of moments, or even hours. Rather, death is an event, like birth. And that makes the process of dying more like the lengthy process of growing.

Taking this idea to the next step, consider that when you came into the world, you had to develop the knowledge and skills necessary for survival. You learned to walk, communicate, control some of your bodily functions, and focus your mind. You saw the world as a fascinating place. You engaged with the world and with those around you with unbridled enthusiasm. Everything was wonderful.

The skills you developed, the relationships you formed, and the gratification you took in your achievements all served to encourage your attachment to the world.

Dying is the same process—in reverse.

Your loved one will lose power and influence in the world. He will lose many symbols of his achievements. He will lose many family and social roles, some very cherished. He will eventually lose the relationship to his body. We will talk more of this in the season of October and November.

Each of these losses and events causes your loved one to withdraw from physical life—to detach, to divest. It has been said that all of the world's pain comes from holding onto that which must be released. In the normal process of disease, the moment of death is preceded, and in some ways defined by this series of smaller cumulative losses, each one serving to loosen one's hold on life. Remember this concept and hold it in your heart as you consider the range of losses your loved one must endure until he takes his final breath.

Loss of Social Role

As the process of dying unfolds, more and more energy must go into maintaining physical homeostasis—the body's innate urge to maintain healthy balance and ultimately, life. Very quickly, few energy reserves remain. Activities your loved one once enjoyed must be relinquished.

As illness chips away at his energy, your loved one's place in the world becomes smaller and more uncertain. Progressively, he may retreat more and more from the external world, perceiving himself as a smaller presence in that world. Sociologists term this "social death."

Throughout life, most people form strong social bonds with friends, with extended family, at work, in church, at school, and with people no one else even knows about. All of these social attachments will be severely strained. Some people can cope well with the issues surrounding dying and are sources of great support. Remember that people are different in their abilities to cope with these issues. Keep the following in mind:

- Many people are afraid of death—their own death and that of their loved ones. These people may not be able to be there for their loved ones in the way they or their loved ones would hope. This is not a reflection of their love (or lack of it); it is only representative of their abilities and limitations. Remember that they too have to deal with this loss. Sometimes there is more than you know going on, and they are not particularly willing to share with you. But they want to participate in the caring for your loved one and their friend on their terms, as much as they can.

- Many of your loved one's friends want to help, but don't know what to say or how to act toward you as the caregiver. Do you want to talk about the illness? Would you rather be distracted? The truth is that as the caregiver, your wishes about this may change daily—even hourly. You will have to let your friends know what you need and that your needs and those of your loved one will change throughout this experience. The most important quality they can bring to this situation (besides their love) is their willingness to be flexible.

- Some people are not talkers; some people are chore-oriented. They can drive your loved one to the doctor, help with the laundry, bring food, and walk the dog. But they can't always articulate their feelings well. Their gestures are the evidence of their love and caring. It may have to be enough.

With that said, the sad fact is that some friendships may fall away when your loved one is dying. People may not be able to cope and may choose to abandon the friendship. None of their reasons, however understandable, can mitigate the pain of a friend's abandonment. This is a tough situation for everyone.

Finding Friendships at the End of Life

Be alert, too, for the miraculous friendships that have been there all the time. Sometimes only a crisis a large as death can uncover a loving relationship that has gone unacknowledged for years. There are angels among us, as Leonard learned just in the nick of time.

Leonard

And then a strange thing happened.

For where the tear had fallen,

A flower grew out of the ground.

—*Margery Williams*

Leonard was a quarrelsome gay man who lived in a tiny studio apartment in the North Beach section of San Francisco. He was prideful. He was fastidious. He was opinionated. Sometimes he was a pain in the neck. He was always entertaining. Leonard was an interior designer with a flair for colors and a special love of antiques. His apartment, though small, was beautifully appointed. He had lived in the same art deco building for over thirty years.

When Leonard was a young man, new to San Francisco, he was prominent in the burgeoning gay social scene. He hosted intimate dinner parties for his friends in the arts. He partied his way through the seventies with a dizzying number of sexual and romantic partners. He never connected with a permanent life partner. "It never seemed important," he said.

In the mid-eighties, the sparkling lifestyle of San Francisco's gay community came to a halt. The specter of AIDS had cast a shadow of sorrow, pain, and great fear throughout the city. The bathhouses closed, parties stopped, and the bright lights and burlesque charm of the Castro district began to feel garish and desperate. Gaunt, wasted men haunted the sidewalks. AIDS hospices sprang up throughout the city.

The conversations in cafes were hushed as men spoke in whispers about T cells, AZT, and medical marijuana. By the time Leonard was diagnosed, he already had full-blown AIDS.

In the spring of 1991, we would sit in large antique rockers in Leonard's front window. We sipped Earl Grey tea and gossiped about the people who passed the window on Broadway. Occasionally, Leonard would share some tidbit about his life.

Leonard's health was failing rapidly. The social worker, Nancy, was trying to help Leonard formulate a care plan that would allow him to stay in his beloved apartment until the end. He received practical support assistance from Shanti, San Francisco's premier AIDS assistance agency, and he had weekly visits from the Visiting Nurse Association. A friend or neighbor who could oversee

Leonard's care on a daily basis was needed. Leonard was an intensely private man. For all his socializing and philandering, he had no close friends.

"What about your neighbors?" Nancy asked. "You've been in this building for over thirty years. Surely there is someone here who could help you."

Leonard shook his head. "No," he insisted. "There is no one."

Nancy knew that Leonard had an upstairs neighbor with whom he was friendly. He had watered her houseplants when she was on vacation.

"What about the lady upstairs?" she asked him. "Didn't you say that she has lived here almost as long as you have?"

Leonard was horrified. He exclaimed, "She's British, for the love of God! If she knew that anyone in the building had AIDS, she'd be on the next plane for London. No. My only hope is to stay out of the hospital."

But Leonard was not able to stay out of the hospital. He developed pneumonia and spent almost a month on a ventilator. By the time Leonard was finally off the respirator his weight had plummeted to under one hundred pounds. He did not have the strength of get out of bed.

"My only hope," he told Nancy, "is to get strong enough to go home."

That also was not to be. Leonard went from the hospital to a nursing home. He struggled valiantly against the ravages of his disease and worked daily with a grueling regimen of physical therapy. Leonard's strength did not return. Finally, Leonard looked at Nancy and said, slowly and sadly, "Now I have no hope."

On Easter Sunday, 1991, Nancy sat at Leonard's bedside and read to him from a children's book she had brought, "The Velveteen Rabbit." It is a story about death and resurrection. Leonard listened patiently and, when she had finished, he smiled weakly.

"I don't get it," he said. "I like it. I just don't get it."

Nancy tried to explain. "It's about hope, Leonard—hope for new life, for better things to come. Do you remember hope?"

Leonard could only shake his head sadly. "No," he whispered hoarsely, "I have no hope."

Soon after this conversation, Leonard was transferred to a hospice house. He never saw his home again. His possessions were sorted and disposed of by strangers. It looked for a while as though Leonard had been right—as though all hope was gone.

The people at the hospice house were kind. Leonard had a small room there, which we crammed full of the things he treasured most. As the days passed, spring became summer, and Leonard slumped into a near-death stupor. He had stopped eating altogether—with one exception. Leonard loved chocolate fudge ice cream. Twice a week, Nancy visited Leonard, stopping on the way at the ice-cream parlor for a pint of Ben and Jerry's chocolate fudge. She would sit at his bedside, spoon-feeding him the ice cream, occasionally reminiscing. But more and more, the time they spent together was silent.

Nancy was vaguely aware that Leonard had another visitor in the afternoon. It was Dorothy, the British woman from his apartment building. Dorothy had noticed Leonard's absence from his apartment, and she had somehow found him here at the hospice house. One day, Nancy ran into Dorothy coming out of Leonard's room. Nancy asked how she had known to look for him at the hospice.

"I always knew about the AIDS," she said. "How could I not know?" Then she said something that Leonard overheard and which completely reframed his life.

"He took in my newspapers and gathered my mail last summer when I went home to England. Leonard has been my best friend for almost thirty years. I love him."

Leonard was very weak; far too weak to be his sardonic self. Too weak even to speak. Occasionally, he would pick up a pencil or pen and try to draw—a hold-over from his days as an interior designer. The last time Nancy saw Leonard, there was a picture that he was working on sitting on his night table. It was a pencil drawing of a hill, a plant, and a small elfin figure.

"How cute!" she said. "It looks like a springtime scene."

Leonard touched her forearm and tried to tell her something, but the words didn't come.

"Don't waste your breath," she told him. "You can tell me about it next week."

Leonard looked irritated and frustrated with her. Perhaps he knew that they would not see each other again.

Nancy got a phone call the following Monday. Leonard had died.

"He left something for you," the nurse told her. "A picture he was working on."

When Nancy went to the hospice to pick up the picture, it was obvious that Leonard had been drawing the Velveteen Rabbit. That's what he had been trying to tell her. Leonard had found friendship and love in the midst of his detachment. Leonard had died with hope. The bitterness of his life had been transformed by the discovery that he had been loved from the beginning.

The VELVETEEN RABBIT

Original text by Margery Williams

Original art by William Nicholson

Many roles change because of a terminal illness. Initially, the changes will be subtle, but as the last day of winter approaches, the changes may become profound. You and your loved ones must be prepared for this, whether your friends stick around or not.

As the loss of social role combines with physical changes, the impact on your loved one's self-esteem is magnified. As said before, it is a difficult time for everyone.

Financial Losses

Eventually, your loved one will be unable to continue with his employment. This is a huge loss, especially for those who define themselves by what they do for a living. What's more, illness is always expensive. Few families are prepared to assume the financial costs of illness—especially when this is the very time when income may suddenly decrease or stop completely. Even the best medical insurance rarely covers the total cost of health care when you aren't terminally ill. Coverage seems to wane when catastrophic or terminal illness arises. There are all kinds of limits to health care insurance coverage, including how much money is allowed to go for treatment, whether specific illnesses are covered, the length of time the individual has been sick, time limits on specialist referrals, and which drugs are covered and at what cost. We have all heard the horror stories about cancer patients suing insurance companies or health maintenance organizations (HMOs) to get the treatment they need. While preferred provider organizations (PPOs) offer more choice in terms of physicians and facilities covered, they usually come with higher premiums and with deductibles and co-payments that can accumulate very quickly.

Then there are expenses for transportation, home health care, and custodial care at home. All of these services can be extremely costly. Home health care is the intermittent monitoring of a registered nurse and/or a physical therapist. Medicare, Medicaid, and most private insurance companies usually have a home-care benefit. Custodial care at home is a different matter. Custodial care is assistance with bathing, feeding, changing bed linens, and providing a safe environment for patients with dementia. This is care that, while absolutely essential, is not medical in nature and is usually delivered by a nursing assistant or home health aide. Your medical insurance generally will not pay for these services. Prices vary by area and discipline, but you can expect to pay between eight and twenty dollars per hour for these services. There is usually a four-hour minimum per day. At some point, your best option may be to see a hospice team social worker so that all available resources in your community can be made available to you.

The family will not only suffer the costs of illness, but also the loss of income if the illness occurs before qualifying for retirement benefits. Many employers carry long-term disability insurance for their employees. If you are not going to be able to return to your employment, be sure to check with the human resources specialist where you work (for many of us, that is simply our boss) to clarify what early retirement or long-term disability benefits you may be entitled to receive. Also remember that most people participated in a state disability program (SDI). This can provide modest income when it is most needed. After one year of disability, your loved one will be eligible for federal benefits, including Social Security Disability Income and Medicare. People on drastically reduced incomes may also be eligible for Medicaid programs to supplement Medicare.

These Medicaid programs will pay for prescription medications and assistance in the home. Regulations vary by state, but these programs are usually administered at the county level. Call your county's department of social services to clarify which benefits you may be eligible for and to initiate services. If you have financial assets, such as stocks, savings accounts, or real estate investments, you should visit an accountant or attorney to make sure they are handled in exactly the way your loved one desires. This may also be a good time to take care of the financial aspects of burial or cremation. Since terminal illness and dying can be financially traumatic, it is painful but wise to help your loved one set up a supportive network and a sound financial plan. Now is the time for seeing your lawyer, your banker, and your accountant—not after your loved one has passed away.

Preparing for the Journey

Dying is about changes, losses, growth, and adventure. As these changes and losses mount and move inexorably inward toward the heart of your loved one's identity, certain physiological and psychological transformations occur. External attachments and identifications fail and fall away. The individual begins to search for a more enduring and authentic sense of what he is. He begins to look at life-completion tasks that will help during the transition to death. These tasks may be as simple as finishing that old chair in the garage or installing a new doorbell. He may want to call up an old enemy and forgive him, or tell him off one last time. The tasks may also be complex, depending on what your loved one needs to do in order to feel that his life is complete. He will be likely to feel the need to complete many projects. It is in these tasks that the discovery, adventure, and growth occur.

And as he continues to die, the final external tasks present themselves. September is a foretaste of what is to come. The experience of September will help prepare him for the journey ahead.

As the primary caregiver, you can assist your loved one with the enormous changes and losses he must endure. You can help him grow and discover in order to allow the process of dying to transcend from an external experience to an internal journey, wherein meaning and significance replaces chaos and fear.

Prepare, for it's a long winding path—for your loved one, for you, and for everyone touched by the changes this death will ignite. Not everyone will travel the same path to the final event, but the material in this book applies to everyone going through the dying process, no matter if death occurs in six months or in six years. There is no right or wrong way; there is no single way. The way in which your loved one lives out death is what you have to work with. Since everyone's response is unique, you must let go of preconceived notions of what it should be like or how you want it to be, and simply be present and accepting of what is.

How to Prepare for the Journey

Part of your role is to accompanying your loved one to the edge, supporting him through the difficult times and celebrating the epiphanies. You are the traveling companion, the witness, and occasionally, the guide. How can you gather your own resources to prepare for this odyssey?

- Reconnect with and practice your spiritual beliefs. Pray. Meditate. Consult with your spiritual leaders. This is the time to nourish your own heart.

- Make time each day to do at least one thing that you love. Read a poem. Sit in a favorite spot in the backyard. Walk your dog. Watch your favorite television show. The more chaotic and demanding the world becomes, the more vital it is to carve out your small amount of personal time.

- Enlist the help of friends and family, or hire a private caregiver to give yourself some respite.

- Learn to pace yourself. Runners know how to do this, as do swimmers. Any undertaking that requires endurance also requires the ability to pace. Know when to sprint and when to fall back. You are in this for the long haul. You can't go full speed ahead from start to finish. You will need time out.

- Be sure you are getting good nutrition. It will be tempting to live on carbo-hydrates and sweets. You may even crave them. But you need all the strength and endurance you can muster. You can't live on fast food.

- Exercise. Take a walk around the block. Jog, if you enjoy it. Swim. Moving your body will help release the anxiety you may be feeling. Mild to moder-ate aerobic exercise will also help release endorphins in your brain, so you really will have more emotional stamina. Remember, this is only the begin-ning of a long journey.

3

OCTOBER AND NOVEMBER: FIRST FROST

But Freddie's summer soon passed.

It vanished on an October night.

He had never felt it so cold.

—*Leo Buscaglia, PhD*
"The Fall of Freddie the Leaf"

Supporting Your Loved One through Changes and Losses

This is the season of the first frost. It can be a chilling time of chaos and fear. The initial physical and psychological losses are beginning to manifest and accumulate.

Life changes color in late autumn. Even the texture of the world feels different. Leaves become dry and brittle. They lose their places on the trees and rain down upon the earth quietly, often unnoticed. Trees stand denuded and stark against the sky. The quality of light changes, too, as the world slowly pivots, turning its back to the sun. It is darker, colder, and a musty dampness begins to settle into the bones.

Even the animals know that winter is coming. Migratory birds fly south—their patterns, like their destinations, etched in life's most secret codes. Squirrels who must face the oncoming winter gather food and prepare shelter.

Your loved one changes, too. He becomes more frail. He may become more somber, and increasingly he may turn, like the earth itself, away from the sunshine. He may look further into the distance and notice the approach of winter. He knows that this season is of his heart. He cannot simply fly away from it. He will stay and weather it. He will gather his strengths about him. This is also the time for you to gather your own personal, emotional, and spiritual resources.

External Physical Changes and Loss of Body Image

One of the changes you will notice during this season is in your loved one's appearance. His physical decline may be difficult for you, but it will challenge the very core of your loved one's sense of himself. His attachment to the physical world and the things that physically define him will undergo radical changes.

Your perception of him and the way you identify with him in the physical world will also change. Again, this is a natural part of the dying process, but it can be one of the most difficult.

Life's biggest identity crisis is the physical decline, or life with a different body: a body that can't do what it used to do. We have spoken about death feeling like an intruder—about the sense of disbelief surrounding physical decline. We identify with our bodies. Our bodies are imprinted by our genetic lines. We look like our families. We are tall or short. We are black or white or Asian or Indian. We have our mother's smile or our father's hands. What is it like to lose your physical self? To see your body change so that you hardly recognize it?

As the loss of social role is combined with physical changes, the impact on your loved one's self-esteem is magnified. Just as he is used to receiving consistent messages from the world, he is also used to receiving consistent messages from or about his body image. He is used to his body and how it looks. For most of us, our bodies change slowly over time, allowing us to adjust to or deny the changes. When health fails, the changes may come quickly and often dramatically. It is frequently difficult—and sometimes impossible—to accept the changes, particularly when terminal illness makes the changes irreversibly progressive.

For men in particular, and increasingly so for women, what you do for a living often defines how you perceive yourself. When the time comes for your loved one to stop working, or to stop "doing his thing," and if he has defined himself only by what he does, then this can be the most difficult time in his seasons of dying.

A patient of ours, Peter, had just such an experience.

Peter

Peter was a dancer. In his youth he had been a stunningly handsome man—slender and dark and mysterious-looking. He had been the headliner at a flamboyant nightclub in San Francisco's Castro district. Sitting in his kitchen on a damp October morning, Peter was anything but handsome. His body was ravaged by his long and losing battle with AIDS. His eyes were sunken deep in their sockets, and his cheekbones jutted out at sharp angles, making Peter's face look almost comedic. He was jaundiced from liver damage, and bald from chemotherapy. Perhaps the hardest change of all was that Peter had lost so much weight that he could no longer wear his dentures.

The man who had danced three shows a night, six nights a week was not able to answer a knock at his door. Peter's nurse found him drinking tea at the kitchen table and looking at old photo albums. She joined him at the table, and they chatted about inconsequential things as he showed her who he "really was." He was really a dancer. See? There he is in his sequined tuxedo and top hat. And there he is, again, doing a Maurice Chevalier number. Shuffling to the sink, Peter caught a glimpse of himself in the reflection from the window. "Who is that guy?" he asked. "Who is that dying old man?"

In this season of dying, the physical changes may have progressed to the point where one's self-image changes. Your loved one probably feels completely alienated from his physical self. Chemotherapy, radiation, hormone therapy, and surgeries to treat such diseases as cancer can be far more disfiguring than the conditions they are meant to treat. This progress of disease or physical change will likely include some loss of function, such as the inability to swallow, or the inability to process food or move it along the bowel due to obstruction.

These physical changes are also usually accompanied by other symptoms and events, such as weakness, coughing episodes, and bouts of depression and self-pity. The work of dying is becoming harder.

In the end, your loved one can feel almost completely disconnected from his body.

Juan

Juan is forty-two years old. He lives in a middle-class southern California suburb with his wife and three young children. He manages a large automobile dealership in the Valley. Juan is an attractive, articulate man with an engaging smile and a friendly manner.

Before he got sick, Juan was a meticulous dresser and very fastidious about his appearance. Juan had a muscular physique and worked out several times a week at the gym to maintain his ideal weight.

Then, quite suddenly, he was admitted to the hospital with acute abdominal pain. He was diagnosed with diverticulitis, a disease of the bowel that can interfere with normal digestive function. Treatment required a surgical procedure called an ileostomy. The surgeon made an opening in Juan's abdominal wall, to which the upper part of his bowel was attached. This resulted in the need for Juan to pass fecal waste through this incision, and into the pouch. The material that drains into this pouch is a very unpleasant green or brown liquid.

Pam was asked to visit Juan while he was in the hospital recuperating from surgery. He was having a hard time adjusting to the changes in his body image. The moment Juan saw Pam in the doorway, he pulled the sheets up to his neck. He did not want her to see what he called "the thing." He couldn't look at it, much less call it by name.

He cringed as they both heard the gurgling from his abdomen and knew that the bag was filling. Juan cleared his throat very loudly in a hopeless attempt to disguise the sound. During Pam's visit with Juan, the enterostomal therapist stopped by to show Juan how to empty and change his pouch.

Pam stayed at Juan's bedside as the therapist went about her work. It was important for Juan to see that other people viewed him as "normal" and that they would not shrink back from him. As the therapist went about changing Juan's pouch, she did her work slowly and she encouraged Juan to participate in his own care. She put the new pouch in his hand, so he would have to touch it. Once in a while, he glanced at it. The therapist told Juan about several different types of pouches and adhesive devices and fittings. She explained the use of chlorophyll tablets to minimize odor. She instructed him on how often the pouch must be changed, and she spoke of sterile technique.

After the therapist had left, Pam spent a few more minutes with Juan. He was shaken and tearful following this stark encounter with his new body. Pam encouraged Juan to talk about his feelings, and she suggested he seek counseling to deal with these huge changes. Before she left, she gave Juan information about a support group called Ostomates. Juan glanced briefly at the brochure and rolled his eyes. He tried to make a joke. "Good God, I'm a freaking Martian. And they want me to join a Martian support group."

Within a few days of Juan's discharge from the hospital, he got a call from Roger, who was the local representative of Ostomates. Despite his initial reluctance, Juan agreed to meet with Roger that afternoon.

They had been chatting in Juan's living room for less than twenty minutes when Roger grinned broadly and offered, "Would you like to see mine?" Juan, who had not yet looked at his own stoma, reluctantly agreed. Seeing Roger's stoma and sensing Roger's ease with the whole issue helped Juan come to terms with his own body changes.

Eventually, Juan returned to his job at the automobile dealership. For the most part, life returned to normal. He still works out regularly. He still has a streak of vanity in his make-up. But in facing a challenge to his self-esteem and learning to accommodate a different version of his physical identity, Juan also learned to appreciate the inherent wholeness of his being as an entity—separate from his body. Juan enjoys a more expanded understanding of who he really is.

Internal Losses: The Loss of Self-Image

Self-image is a synthesis of how we see ourselves physically, spiritually, and in the world. It is an outgrowth of our roles in our families, at work, and in our communities. It is a global concept of self. As death changes us and takes away the familiar identifications, we have a great need to identify and connect to different definitions of who we are. We have seen how changes in physical appearance affect the mind and body. The external changes, such as physical appearance and loss of body function, lead to internal changes and the loss of self-image.

Ed's story, which follows, again speaks not only to the loss of body image but to the total loss of identity that can come with physical changes from illness and approaching death.

Ed

Ed was the high school counselor in the small town where he had lived virtually all of his adult life. In the beginning of his career, he had come to the school as a new graduate, a shy and somewhat awkward math teacher. As his initial discomfort with the students abated, young people began to gravitate to his classroom. Ed was the youngest teacher at the high school, and the kids began to seek out his assistance with their academic problems and his advice on more personal matters.

Over the years, his relationship with the students, and ultimately his role at the school, expanded and changed to that of school counselor, which he loved. It was so much more personally gratifying than teaching math. Years passed. Hundreds of students—one kid at a time—benefited from Ed's warmth and guidance. Ed did not make a lot of money, but he had a rewarding, secure, and very successful career. He couldn't go anywhere in the town without running into one of his students. Being the high school counselor was more than just what he did. It was an enormous piece of how Ed perceived himself. It was who he was.

When Ed's emphysema became too advanced for him to continue at the high school, he fell into a very deep depression and seriously considered suicide.

Sitting on the back porch of his house, lighting a cigarette, he remarked to the social worker who was visiting, "Now what am I?" He took a deep drag on the cigarette, coughed, and looked over at her. She could only stare dumbly at her lap as he asked again, "Now what am I?"

What can you do to help your loved one as he struggles with feelings of alienation from his body? You cannot stop the onslaught of feelings or pain. You may only share them and mitigate them. You may share that sense of strangeness with his diminishing health and the disintegration of his body. You must, however, keep in your heart the heart's own image of whom you loved all these years: his love of poetry; his gentleness with old people; his sense of humor. These are the qualities that will endure. Remind him of them. And remind yourself of them. In the end, these are the qualities that will reappear and sustain you both in the midst of all of this decay. These are the qualities, in the end, that will save him. And save you.

Loss of Safety

Behind him lay the gray Azores

Behind the Gates of Hercules

Before him not the host of shores

Before him only shore-less seas.

—*Joaquin Miller*

When training hospice volunteers to work with patients and families, we do an exercise with them to help them access their own inherent responses to personal loss. In this exercise, we pass out brightly colored construction paper, felt pens, glitter, scissors, and glue stick and ask them to work with us in creating their personal mandalas (focus points) to represent their worlds. They each select six pieces of colored paper. On each piece of paper, they are to write a bit of information about themselves and their worlds.

1. What they do for a living, or what they do in the world

2. The thing they like most about themselves: a "one-word advertisement"

3. The name of someone they love

4. Something they love to do

5. Someone else they love

6. Their most dearly held dream or fantasy of their future.

After they have completed this task, we ask them to arrange each piece of paper in a pattern on poster-sized construction paper. Then, using the felt pens, glitter, glue, and scissors, they take these snippets of their lives and create their own mandalas. We ask them not to glue the pieces down permanently, but to put a dab of glue stick on each piece—just enough to hold the mandala together while they're discussing it with the group.

At first, there is a lot of resistance to this exercise: much groaning and references to touchy-feely stuff. It is always gratifying to watch their enthusiasm grow as they arrange the stuff of their lives, placing it just so on the paper.

They reach for the glitter to highlight the really important areas. They use the felt pens for emphasis. They carefully tear or cut the shapes and struggle with placement, pattern, and color. They sometimes chat and socialize happily as they go about their work. Other times, the room is silent and the air is heavy with portent. Finally, they complete their task, visibly pleased with the products of their work.

Next, we go around the table asking them to introduce themselves to us using the mandalas as their life maps. "Tell us about the mandala," we ask them. "Tell us who you love and what gives you joy and what you do in the world. Tell us your dream." They share their mandalas with laughter and sometimes tears.

"This is my dog," one woman said. "He's a person to me, and I love him best in the world."

"This says 'Doctor,'" a young woman tells us. "I was just accepted into Stanford Medical School. I don't even want to think about how much money I'll be borrowing for this, but I don't care. I have wanted to be a doctor since I was eight."

A middle-aged man blushes a little and says, "My favorite thing about myself is my pecs." His blush deepens as the room dissolves in laughter, "I know, I *know*," he protests, laughing a little himself. "But it's *true*."

And so it goes, around the table, people sharing intimate bits of themselves with this room full of strangers, exposing themselves, being vulnerable, but feeling safe.

As the presentations come to a close, we ask them to make any last-minute adjustments to their life maps. Usually, there is little more to be done. Then we ask once more if they're ready to glue the pieces in place. They nod confidently.

"Well," we say (still smiling), "that's a little like how real life works. Just when you have everything where you want it, life comes along and takes something away from you." At that point, we take off our glasses and walk around the table, stopping at each person's mandala. Without a word, we cruelly remove one or more of their pieces. Justice is blind, they are told, and without our glasses, so are we. We have no idea what piece is being pulled. We only see the colored paper coming up from the landscape of their lives. What we don't see, we do hear.

"You took my husband!" a woman cries out.

"No," protests the young woman, "not medical school!"

Still others sigh in relief as I walk away with "blue eyes" or "roller-blading."

We break for fifteen minutes immediately after this exercise, and then come back together to process reactions to it. Invariably, there is anger. They are left with ugly holes in their creations. There was no warning and there was no logic to what was taken from them. As we process their response to this exercise, they are reminded that this is only a game we are playing. They know that this is only a paper world. Yet their responses are real and painful.

For patients and their families, this is not paper. This is how the world looks. This is how their hearts feel. Life really did come up behind them and take away something or someone that made their world complete. And now their lives are scarred and dotted with holes. After we have processed the exercise, we have a break for lunch so we can prepare and rest for the lecture portion of the training in the afternoon.

One afternoon after doing this exercise, we became aware of a sense of uneasiness. It persisted throughout various subsequent classes, no matter how the material was organized or how we altered the presentation. Something felt *wrong*, and it was difficult to put a finger on it. After several sessions, we confronted the problem directly. We were discussing Kubler-Ross and the stages of grief, but it was clear that the class was not connecting with the subject or us.

We stopped the lecture and asked them, "What's wrong here? Is something not clear? Does something not make sense?"

They looked at us uncomfortably. Finally an older man in the back of the room stood up and said, "Okay, we just want to know what you're *really* going to do this afternoon."

We were perplexed. What was he talking about? He continued, "The mandala thing seems to be over. We're just waiting to see what you're going to do to us now."

So there it was. They no longer trusted us. We had misled them and betrayed their trust just that morning. Now everything we did and said was suspect. They could not relax in our presence. Their feelings of openness and safety had vanished with those hastily snatched bits of paper. That feeling would not be easily rekindled.

We no longer approach life in a casual, intimate, carefree way. Life is no longer our chum; it is the dowager come to tea. When we begin to interact with the world, we do it with caution, with great emphasis on the structure and little investment in the process itself. In that same vein, the afternoon classes were watching us closely, but they were not willing to invest in us at the moment.

The students in our afternoon classes were sitting uncomfortably, waiting for the other shoe to drop. Like those whose life losses are real, they were vigilant: ready, this time. In the world of the dying, innocence and vulnerability seem to be gone forever, no longer valid, no longer even desired. Joy itself, vulnerability itself, trust itself—these become the enemy. Reflecting on what goes on in real-life scenarios of loss, the trainees were so outraged by the deceit that they didn't want to trust us.

No matter how prepared we feel ourselves to be, the loss of a loved one is jarring. The unthinkable has happened. In an instant, not just our world, but our status in that world is forever altered. And, like the paper mandalas, we are left torn and diminished and afraid. Whether immediately or more gradually, the sense of betrayal and mistrust emerges.

A former patient, now in remission from breast cancer, said it this way: "When I was diagnosed with cancer, it was as though I lost citizenship in life itself. Now it feels like I'm here on a temporary visa that's about to expire."

Trust Versus Control

Feelings of loss occur for both the one dying, and for those who care for her. In some cases, the feelings of insecurity are too frightening to be felt, processed, and released. In an attempt to banish the fearfulness of living in a random universe, there is often an impotent grasp for control.

Mrs. Murray

Mrs. Murray's husband of thirty-seven years had a sudden heart attack at the dinner table. The paramedics were called, and they responded quickly. Thankfully, Mr. Murray made it to the hospital in time to be saved. He was well on the way to mending before the care team could turn its attention to his wife, who was present every day.

Mrs. Murray had brought food from home every day, insisting that the hospital food was not nutritious enough. She maintained a vigil in her husband's room, watching the monitors constantly. The nurses called our office and asked that the social worker speak with Mrs. Murray about her husband's need for sleep and time to be alone, as well as about our nurses' time to care for him.

"But I have to watch the monitors, "Mrs. Murray protested. "What if his heart stops?"

The social worker tried to reassure her that such an event would set off many alarms. She showed Mrs. Murray the monitoring equipment at the nursing station and the crash cart and equipment. She carefully explained our intensive care unit (ICU) emergency and cardio-pulmonary resuscitation (CPR) procedures. Mrs. Murray was not impressed.

"What if your monitors don't work?" she asked. "I think I'll just stay here again tonight."

Mr. Murray's heart attack had robbed his wife of her sense of safety in the world. Her hyper-vigilance in the ICU caused her to be seen by the staff as a dysfunctional woman with control issues. However, Mrs. Murray was only trying to re-establish some sense of sanity and security. The world could no longer be trusted. She could no longer trust her own dining room table—how could she trust these nurses, who were strangers until a few days ago? Mrs. Murray's fearfulness and distrust emerged immediately.

Sometimes these feelings lie dormant until after a crisis passes, and are labeled post-traumatic stress disorder.

Sometimes the life changes induced by a life-threatening diagnosis can make you or your loved ones behave in unexpected ways—contrary to the expectations of others. The story of Margaret is a poignant example of this concept.

Margaret

Margaret is a forty-nine-year-old woman who now lives in a Florida suburb. Ten years ago, her children were approaching independence, and she decided to return to college. She had a successful and meaningful career and had raised three wonderful children to near-adulthood. The opportunity to go back to college and complete her long-ago-interrupted education seemed like a dream come true. "This is my go at it," she said as she started her classes.

Margaret worked very hard at her studies, did well scholastically, and was seriously thinking of graduate school. She even bought a new car—a red Chrysler New Yorker. It seemed to fit her new image and her new life.

Four months before Margaret was to graduate from college and receive her degree, she was diagnosed with an inoperable brain tumor. It came out of nowhere. She'd noticed a few headaches, a little blurred vision and vertigo upon arising. The news was devastating. Margaret initially met the shock and bewilderment with her well-honed sense of humor. She would smile wryly, point her finger pistol-style to her head, and chant, "Bing, bang, boom—you're dead."

Only Margaret wasn't dead. She underwent a grueling course of radiation therapy that left her nauseous and debilitated and weak. We watched and supported her, and cheered as the tumor shrank. Two years later, there was no sign of the tumor. And there was no sign of Margaret.

She sold the red Chrysler, and bought a gray economy sedan. At the insistence of her friends and family, she completed her degree, but she neither applied for graduate school nor went back to her career.

She stayed home day after day, renting videos of old movies from the 1950s. This woman, who had been active and vital, overflowing with plans, goals, and enthusiasm for life, began to shrink back from the world.

"I was afraid," she says now. "It's hard to explain. It was like I was out there, doing things I love, and then God said, 'Bing, bang, boom—you're dead.' After that, I just wanted to hide. And I didn't want God to see me." For Margaret, life itself had become the thing to be feared. "I didn't want God to see me."

When the unthinkable happens, all assumptions about safety in the world are called into question. The ground is no longer solid beneath the feet. Trusting others no longer comes easily. Trusting oneself is difficult, as is trusting life itself. This loss of trust and feelings of safety may manifest itself in a struggle for control, as in Mrs. Murray's case, or in a retreat from the world, as in Margaret's situation. There may be other behavioral or psychological symptoms, but the way in which they are presented does not matter.

What does matter is that, to someone who is dying, the world has shattered. At this critical point, your loved one must renegotiate her contract with life. Feelings of insecurity manifest through many different physical and psychological losses. Typically, she will never experience certainty again.

Something's Lost, but Something's Gained

Psychologists refer to the unexpected benefits that emerge from painful times or difficult events as "compensatory gains." This process also occurs after an individual loses his sense of safety. When the world stops shaking beneath his feet, he sometimes notices something different about himself. After he wrestles with confusion and terror, after he staggers across the landscape of fear, he notices a huge shift in the way he experiences himself and his life. He knows that the outcome is unpredictable. With that knowledge comes the loosening of attachment to outcomes, and a greater ability to live his life in the present.

If he survives this harrowing experience, there is great potential for transformation that can enhance his experience of life, however long or short the remainder of his life may be. The decisions he makes, the priorities that he establishes, and the qualities of commitment and passion that he brings to his life undergo a huge change. The crisis that precipitated the loss of safety becomes a watershed event. From that time forward, it will exist as a major marker from which the rest of his life is gauged. As your loved one's caregiver, it's important to understand this.

The transit through the loss of safety reminds us at the deepest levels of our souls that guarantees do not exist, especially guarantees about our health and future lives. Walking this path with someone you love will evoke your own feelings of vulnerability. To lose someone you love is to relinquish some of your own hold on life. And it reminds us that when we are healthy—any of us—we are simply in our disease-free intervals. This acknowledgment of our own mortality imparts a particular kind of freedom to experience the present.

Well Worn

Time is making me

Less afraid

Of scars and stains,

More appreciative

Of the hard and soft

People and things

Around me,

More willing

To risk everything

To be well worn

And pleasantly used

Before I outgrow

this life.

—*Patrick W. Flanigan, MD*

Life Review

I remember

the edges of pain being sharper

the climate of the spirit

autumn morning crisp

the sound of my breath

more sacred/more profane

and now

the November of the soul roars in

a crush of ashen foliage

and I remember.

—*Carrie Hyde*

Resolution, acknowledgment, and acceptance occur as life review and dying progresses. This is the time when important questions are asked, and answers are sought. Life review will be ongoing from this time until the end. Your loved one will be looking back across his days for meaning and purpose. He will be approaching the end of this dynamic relationship he has with the world and with those he loves—including you.

You are coming to an ending, too: the end of your life with your loved one. You will also look back across the landscape of your time together. You will reflect, balance, and decipher the meaning of your life together and your part in sharing his death. This is where you and your loved one begin to find out how things end up, and start coming to terms with what is happening. It is the beginning of your ability, in the end, to say good-bye.

In "Journey to Ixtlan," Carlos Castaneda reminds us that death guides us if we heed his counsel: "Death is our counselor, sitting just over our shoulder, whispering gently in our ear."

Death tells us what is important, what we need to do next, and what we can put away. In heeding this counsel, we will open up to all the possibilities of life.

In accompanying our loved ones as they face death, we *all* can open up for more possibilities of life.

The role of a caregiver in communication with a dying loved one is critically important, whether it is a professional caregiver (nurse, physician, social worker), a family member, or a beloved friend. Most important are the needs of your dying loved one, and more specifically, the spiritual needs common to all people at the end of life. If everyone—professional caregivers, friends, and family—is aware of these common concerns, then communication with the loved one is more effective.

As we have said, physical limitations will force your loved one to accept the progress of the disease and to acknowledge that it will move inexorably toward death. This is a slow but steadily progressive process.

The emotional response to this confrontation with personal mortality can be very strong, and the dying one will probably vent on those who are both physically and psychologically closest to him. The target of the individual's emotions may be family, friends, a lover, the doctor or other caregivers, or even God. It is important for everyone to understand that these emotional expressions are not meant as personal attacks, but rather are reflective of the underlying emotional crisis precipitated by the experience of dying itself. These emotional expressions need to be allowed, understood, and accepted in order to facilitate the patient's emotional investment and ongoing participation in the living/dying process. The loved one is, in this way, becoming the guide to those who will love, nurture, and relinquish him—and who will ultimately follow him in death. His positive self-image is reinforced by the knowledge that his experiences are valued and respected, which is your task. This is not easy in the face of what seems to be abuse by your dying loved one. Be strong. You are not only capable of doing this, but you are capable of doing more than you think. You can do this. And of course, you will do so, with great success.

Actually, life review begins in one form or another as soon as the diagnosis of a terminal illness is made. It may be subconscious for some time, but it is ongoing nevertheless. The process becomes more active and evident the closer a person perceives himself to dying. Be aware that this process will be ongoing until the final breath. There are many loose ends to bring together in each life.

Understanding the Concepts of Life Review

The process of life review is both important and fascinating. It serves to create a concept of self that is crucial to a complete dying process. Your loved one will remember his life. The memories coming from sensory, auditory, and fantasy input emerge spontaneously. They can come in the middle of the afternoon, or in the middle of a conversation. They come from external cues: a fragrance vaguely remembered, the light through the window shades, the sound of a particular voice. They can also come from within the depths of mind and memory. These flashes of memory increase in frequency and vividness as death nears. A person brings to his death all of the collective memories and experiences of his life: The triumphs and the failures, the first dance, the first kiss, the first disappointment—they are all there. Like a good story, a life also has a beginning, a middle, and an ending.

One of the life-review tasks of your dying loved one is to revisit these fragments of meaning and the seemingly random experiences of earlier times. In life review, these bits and pieces of experience strewn across our days like cast-off pebbles are brought together and reexamined. There can be a reorganization of accomplishments, a new assignment of meanings, a shift in priorities. Self-concept emerges renewed from life review. A new perspective on the patient's life is achieved by the patient himself, and by those with whom he may share his journey. Therefore, death can take its place in the context of the patient's life as an acceptable transition. It was a life well-lived.

As death approaches, life review continues. Life review allows you, as well as your loved one, a way to conceptualize the entirety of life and a way to understand and contain the presence of pain. In understanding life in its wholeness, suffering is given the boundaries of context. Life review may lead to a deeper understanding of the relationship between your loved one's suffering and the manner in which death is faced.

Helping Your Loved One with Life Review

The most valuable gift you can give to your loved one during his review of life is to listen. Let him know you are there to witness his life and to hear the entirety of his story. There will be parts of this story that include your relationship with him. You can help him and yourself by participating in these walks down memory lane. Some of the memories will be wonderful and will bring you closer together: the memory of the day you met; birthdays, perhaps; anniversaries. These are the important days in your ongoing story.

Not all memories will be easy for you to hear and process. Long-standing relationships often go through difficult and painful times. What's more, the two of you may see some issues and times in very different ways. It is important that you hear what your loved one is saying. This does not mean you need to agree with his version of the story—only that you do not negate his way of experiencing it. Listen with the intent to understand—not to correct. Sometimes, you will listen quietly; other times, the discussion may be lively.

Not all memories will include you. Not all memories will be pleasant to you. Your loved one may have a child he cherishes who is not your child and whom you do not love. He may have friends you have never enjoyed or approved of. Although you have been close and loving, it is good to remember that each person's life comprises a broad landscape. It encompasses many experiences, many people, and many types of passion. You cannot possibly be center stage in each discrete nuance.

People bring to the last days of their lives memories and images that were intrinsic to the formation of their characters and the experiences of their lives. If you were to string together everything in life that was meaningful, it might last less than a year. The rest of the time just seems like we are all *standing in line*. What matters in the end is how much time is spent doing the meaningful things, not how much time one stayed on the planet or stood in line. Your loved one will focus on these important times in his life. The issues that we see as important when we are in the middle of our productive years may seem less significant in the end.

Life review is all about recapturing the meanings of these moments. It culminates in allowing those moments to go and relegating them to a very individual priority list. The process allows letting go and accomplishing acceptance and acknowledgment. These will let your loved one open his mind so the miracles of December can happen.

> Life review is a culmination of allowing and letting go. It is the time when the unrelated fragments of life are brought together. Dr. Eric Cassell, a famous British terminal care physician, talks of the "topology of the person." This idea may be useful in helping your loved one, but everyone must choose the way that is useful for their own situation. Here is a summary of Cassell's ideas, and we present them to you for consideration.
>
> • During life review, your loved one examines his **past**. He revisits what he has accomplished, when he has failed, and what is left undone. He recalls places he's visited, and places left for another time. These experiences are a part of yesterday, today, and tomorrow. Events of the present can modify and impact the memories of the past, and new meanings can be assigned to events that took place in a far different time and place. An important gift of life review is that all of the fragments of an individual's life—including

secret lives—will come together as a cohesive whole and offer peace and calm. As your loved one goes through this process, be supportive and loving. Try not to be judgmental, and allow the flow of memories to go unfettered, without critical comment.

- **Memories** also play into topology and reveal how your loved one's life was colored and intensified. Some memories once thought pivotal are dismissed and buried in the flow. For example, a successful business executive may reflect with great happiness and pride on his first "real" job, and that first raise (to $5.00 an hour) may be a greater source of pride and satisfaction to him than the stock options he later enjoyed. An elderly homemaker who appears to have led a small and passionless existence may carry memories of her first dance and her first love that she holds secretly in her heart…embarrassed for the rest of us to guess the feelings she has known. A mechanic lying on his deathbed, gazing out the window, may be reliving the day he caught the ball and saved the game for his team—the day he became the hometown hero for just one moment's time—or the day he *almost* caught the ball. Memories are stored in our senses. The smell of freshly cut grass can evoke memories of long childhood summers. Hospital smells can jar us back to a terrifying experience involving stitches. Hands have memories of their own and ignite even more images: washing dishes in scalding water, soothing a frightened child, rebuilding the engine on a '57 Chevy. Feet remember the awkward feel of ski boots that first time—and the exhilarating slippery feeling of flying down the mountain. Legs and arms still remember the fatigue of carrying a crying baby all night long when she had colic. Memories are stored in our senses. And our bodies remember.

- **Life experiences with health** and previous illnesses, interactions with doctors, caregivers, drugs, hospitals, surgeries, disabilities, and so much more form the background and references for the present illness and responses to it. If your loved one has successfully overcome illness in the past, the current terminal disease is viewed from a more optimistic and stronger perspective. Hence, while his body may be dying, he does not perceive of himself as dying as an entity. His good experiences with previous illnesses can give him strength and confidence to negotiate the disease of today. Likewise, if he has not had good health and has been battling illness of one kind or another most of his life, this will influence his perception and experience of the present disease.

- Topology also includes reviewing **family relationships**. People often view themselves as extensions of their parents. In death, their perceptions are often affected by memories of their parents' deaths. Family identity can influence the style that a patient employs to bear suffering. The family identity also aids in acceptance of a fatal or terminal disease process. Cassell points out that the disease becomes the ultimate connection to the family—destiny is being fulfilled. Just as your loved one's personal past gives meaning to his present experiences, so does the collective past of his family contribute to his present reality. His experience as an individual must be integrated with his experience of himself as a member of his family to complete his new and reformulated self-concept. A friend of ours has a lot of heart disease in his family. His mother and everyone on his mother's side of the family died from heart attacks in very advanced years. He was sure that he too would die of a heart attack—preferably after his ninetieth birthday. But when he was in his early seventies, his doctor diagnosed him with Lou Gehrig's disease. His sense of fear and sadness was coupled with a kind of outrage. This wasn't supposed to happen to him. He was supposed to die of heart disease. It was a family tradition.

- **State of mind** is another component of topology. Your loved one has identified himself and has been identified by others through what becomes predictable behavior. We all do this, and it is based on history. But death is so rattling that these predictable behaviors change. For example, someone typically stoic can become needy. A nurturing person may suddenly go inward and want solitude. You may think you know the person, but these changes can make you feel as though you no longer know your loved one. In fact, these changes are simply illustrating more of who he is. By accepting these changes, your embrace of and love for the other grows and expands.

- During this time, your loved one's **physical body** will play a significant role in his self-concept. Very few of us see our bodies as tissue that is useful only in supporting our minds. We tend to identify strongly with our body images. Our bodies carry the physical features of our genetic line. Perhaps you have "your mother's eyes." Perhaps you have "your father's hair." Once, years ago, while Pam was piloting a cabin cruiser on San Francisco Bay, she looked at her hands on the helm and realized with a start that she had her father's hands! Her father had been dead for ten years, but for a brief second on that sunny day on the bay, they were connected. Pam's connection to him was in her body. Your loved one's relationship to his body, his perception of his body, and his attachment to his body will influence how he copes with the process of terminal illness. The body will change, will lose vitality, will become increasingly less attractive and useful, and will ultimately be relinquished. As death approaches, the body may be viewed as failing him. This perception of failure by the body must also be addressed and resolved. This is a most important component of the healing that must be accomplished in the life review process. It is completed by acceptance and acknowledgment.

- Everyone has a **secret life**. This may take the form of fantasies or dreams or, on occasion, a real existence known only to a few. This secret life may contain lives and loves of the past and present, perhaps a secret profession, a unique way of problem-solving known only to the patient, or deeply held emotional issues. Cassell holds that it is appropriate that these remain secret as part of a very private and separate life. Unfortunately, a terminal illness affects everyone involved—including those with whom your loved one shared a secret relationship. There is tragedy in that the dying person cannot offer a legitimate place at the deathbed to a secret lover, friend, or associate because in the public life, there is no legitimate place. Not being able to share the experience of dying with the secret love or friend can profoundly impact your loved one and his or her dying process. This may explain an otherwise inexplicable act or behavior. He or she may now have lost a part of life that made tolerable a host of embittered relationships or situations. This important relationship cannot become an open part of your loved one's life review unless the secret life becomes known and is accepted by the family and other loved ones.

- The perceived **future** must also be reviewed. This is a future for your children and grandchildren, other family, friends, even secret parts of your life. It can be as banal as what will happen to the estate, or as pressing as who will care for a beloved pet. Personal issues are the pressing concerns. If you loved one can envision a positive future for your family and children, it can bring a sense of hopefulness to his final transition. Hope has been mentioned many times as a trait necessary to a successful life. Alisdair MacIntyre, an Irish poet, gives us a different definition of hope, and we offer it to you and your loved one as support for your journey through life review: "Hope is in place precisely in the face of evil that tempts us to despair, and more especially that evil that belongs specifically to our own age and condition…The presupposition of hope is, therefore, belief in a reality that transcends what is available as evidence."

- The last area of life review we will share with you and your loved one is the **transcendent dimension** of the person. This is a life of the spirit, however it is expressed or acknowledged. We know precious little about what transcendence is, given the central place it occupies in our religious belief systems, in the relief of suffering, and in our overall lives. When we speak of the transcendental self, we are referring to that part of us that survives the death of our bodies and supercedes our actions and deeds on earth. Many people believe in an enduring soul, perhaps a soul that returns to human life in many different times and circumstances. Others believe in a spiritual afterlife: a heaven or a hell. Some people feel that life ceases in all its forms with physical death. But we all agree on the endurance of memory. No matter what other forms we may continue to exist in, we will always exist within and have impact on the unfolding lives of those who have loved us.

Cassell states that help is found in the mystic tradition, both inside and outside of traditional religion. Your dying loved one may achieve the sense of his own eternal existence if he can identify with an entity or quality that transcends or goes beyond our finite definition of life. This journey is necessary for your loved one because it prepares her for an emerging perspective that will take her beyond the bounds of suffering, illness, and physicality. The idea is that we are spiritual beings having physical experiences. The journey will take many forms, and it has no timetable.

But in that sleep of death what dreams may come

when we have shuffled off this mortal coil…

—*William Shakespeare*

Life review has not necessarily been completed as your loved one is actively dying and nearing death. Remember, it's ongoing. Your loved one knows this and determines the timetable. Everyone has different life review needs.

The Beginning of the Grief Process

November has come, and therefore it is time for everyone to grieve. Grieving is ongoing, and it is something that you and your loved one will *do*. It is the expression in the world of our profound sorrow and sense of loss. It has probably been ongoing for some time for everyone close to your loved one. Remember, the things we talk about are fluid and can be going on at the same time—and not necessarily in the order in which we share them with you. Everyone's deaths and circumstances are different. Use the knowledge we share to place it in your own situation.

People grieve differently, and it is important to respect those differences and to acknowledge the integrity of each person's process. Many people express their grief through rituals and ceremonies of religion. They light candles, they sit shivah, they celebrate masses, they pray, or they meditate. The support of a spiritual leader—a minister, priest, mullah, or rabbi—is often comforting.

Some people grieve openly and verbally. They seek support from family, close friends, or professional counselors. They talk about their feelings. They cry. They reach out physically, clutching a reassuring hand, collapsing into a warm embrace. They seek connection and intimacy with others in the world. Although it is difficult to work with the fear and pain of a dying loved one, it is often easier for some people to bear when they express themselves verbally and share their inner worlds.

Other people don't do that. They grieve more quietly. We have said that people usually die the way they live. In like manner, people grieve in a way that is consistent with the way they have handled other losses in life.

Aside from our individual differences, there are significant cultural differences in the way we express grief. Some cultures are more introspective than others. Feelings are shared, and thoughts are expressed in mutually understood gestures and nuances. The traditions, fixed relationships, and norms of the family and community provide structure for grief and for healing. Your presence will comfort your loved one even if his grieving remains internal. And your respect of his personal and cultural way of grieving will provide relief and refuge.

A very young woman who was dying of cancer came to our support group one night. She was silent during the meeting, and after it was over, she asked if we would stay with her for a few moments. When everyone had left, we sat expectantly, thinking that now that she was alone with us she would want to process her feelings. She said, "I don't want to talk. I just want you to sit here with me." We sat in silence for several minutes. Then she said, "I'm okay now. I'm going home."

Several weeks later, she called on the phone. She told us that she didn't want to be part of a support group; she was too private a person. It didn't feel natural or comfortable to her. Before she hung up, she said, "But that night we met, I was in a cave. You didn't make me come out. You came into the cave with me. You shared the silence and the dark and the fear. For the first time in a long time, I didn't feel alone. Thank you."

The feelings we talk about are universal, but their expression is deeply personal. Whatever you or your loved one is feeling, and whatever the mechanism of expression may be, it is your presence that makes the difference—your willingness to be there.

Dealing with Anger

Do not go gentle into that good night

Old age should burn and rave at close of day;

Rage, rage against the dying of the light.

—*Dylan Thomas*

"What kind of god would allow this to happen?"

Anger is the first show of direct resistance to what is happening. No matter how hard your loved one looked the other way, this terrible disease just wouldn't leave, and God didn't seem to help. Chances are, you are *all* angry. You are angry with the doctors for not catching it sooner, or for not being able to cure your loved one. You are angry with the nurses for not responding fast enough to the call light, for not finding the vein on the first stick, for shining the flashlight in the eyes of your loved one at three o'clock in the morning. You are angry at the social worker for being unable to take away your sorrow, for missing your call yesterday, and for being so damned chirpy. This is not pleasant, but it's normal—to be expected, in fact. It is healthy and must be honored as part of the process of letting go.

Spring

To what purpose, April, do you return again?

Beauty is not enough.

You can no longer quiet me with the redness

Of little leaves opening stickily.

I know what I know.

The sun is hot on my neck as I observe

The spikes of the crocus.

The smell of the earth is good.

It is apparent that there is no death.

But what does that signify?

Not only underground are the brains of men

Eaten by maggots.

Life in itself is nothing.

An empty cup, a flight of uncarpeted stairs.

It is not enough that yearly, down this hill

April

Comes like an idiot, babbling and strewing flowers.

—*Edna St. Vincent Millay*

In railing against spring, Millay expresses not just her anger, but also her indignation about the unfairness of what has happened. She addresses her loss in a proactive and energetic manner: "You can no longer quiet me. I know what I know."

In expressing her displeasure with the world, Millay gains ascendancy over the circumstances of her existence. This is important! She levels the criticism, and demands that the world respect her. "It is not enough," she says to the seasons. The potency of her anger restores her sense of competency and dignity in the world. This demonstrates why anger is healthy during this time.

In the same way, your loved one will likely express his anger and outrage at this assault upon his existence in order to, in essence, reassert his sense of entitlement. This can be a difficult passage for you and other caregivers because you will often be (or feel as though you are) the target of generalized anger. Since this can be a painful time, you may urge him to return to "normal," or to emotional homeostasis. Bear in mind, however, that the dying loved one needs the infusion of energy that is released with rage.

It might help to remember that even though you may be the recipient of the anger, you are not the target of the anger. It is almost never about you personally, or about your personal relationship with your loved one. The anger is his. It is an emotional response to what is happening to him.

A critical source of this emotion is the anger your loved one may feel with himself, possibly relating to lifestyle choices that he feels may have contributed to his medical problems and the current state of affairs. He may feel angry about missed opportunities in life, angry about failed relationships, or angry for not having acted on his heart's longings. He sees the last page of his life being written, and he is not satisfied with the story of his life. The anger he feels may also be expressed in prayers to his god. He may perceive that he has been abandoned by God and express anger about this. "Surely, this must be an uncaring God if I am allowed to die before my time. Why are *you* allowing this to happen to me?"

This anger will act as an impetus, giving him a renewed sense of urgency and the energy to act. He picks up the reins of his life, with purpose this time, and with intention. The gift of anger is self-determination.

Assuming the Suffering

The terminal patient and those who love and care for him often speak of a profound sense of isolation from each other despite the fact that everyone needs and seeks enhanced communication. If the caregiver can enable better, clearer, more loving communication, those involved will be able to say what must be said to each other before death occurs.

This is a time when fear resides deeply within everyone—fear of the unknown, fear of pain, fear of not being brave enough to see the journey through, fear of abandonment by other family members and friends. Everyone fears that the loved one may die alone, and that they may not be there for this terminal event. This is the time for you to draw as closely as possible to the loved one, reassuring him that he need not face and endure death alone.

How can you best assist in this process of transformation, this going from life to death? Ira Byock, MD, a well-known palliative care physician, uses a poem by Rainer Maria Rilke to explain the mindset of the dying person whose suffering surpasses physical distress. The poem is really a prayer to Rilke's god, but can easily become the plea of the newly diagnosed terminal and dying patient who is trying to communicate with his caregivers and to you.

It's possible that I am pushing through solid rock in flint-like

layers as the ore lies, alone: I am such a long way in, I see no

way through, and no space: Everything is close to my face,

and everything close to my face is stone.

I don't have much knowledge yet with the grief—

So this darkness makes me feel small.

You be the master: Make yourself fierce, break in!

Then your great transformation will happen to me,

and my great cry of grief will happen to you.

—*Rainer Maria Rilke*

If you choose to follow Rilke's lead, you will assume some of the suffering and emotional pain of your loved one. Rilke is asking you to go to the one dying and help transform him by sharing the pain and emotional turmoil. Rilke says you need to understand the pain and emotional turmoil in such a way that the dying one *feels* you have accomplished this, and that it is of primary importance. By doing this, your loved one is not alone, and his suffering can be eased.

Byock says that this concept of Rilke's is the root of compassion, and that through compassion, a magnificent transformation is possible. Byock goes on to suggest that this precarious work, this beckoning of intimacy, can lead to disabling fear in caregivers. Doctors, by the way, are not immune to that fear. Doctors sometimes use labels like "intractable" to describe a person's pain and suffering. "Intractable?" says Byock. "Is this not the same as giving up? It is easier to say, 'I can't help.' If you along with us, as family and caregivers, are to continue to transform, you must all act beyond our knowledge, you must all feel your way through the darkness."

Rilke gives the ultimate task to the caregiver: the sharing of the pain and suffering of the dying loved one, acting honestly and compassionately, without reliance on psychological formulas or "cookbook medicine." No acting. Nothing phony. Feel your way in the dark to accompany your loved one on his journey. By undergoing the transformation as Rilke asks, you can help facilitate a living death. There is no greater commitment or undertaking—or one that requires more courage—than to acknowledge the ultimate *unknowing*.

The realization and acceptance that you and your loved one are going down this unknown path towards death together creates a strong base from which to delve into the unknowing. The feeling that neither of you is alone—that you are together in this experience—is a huge comfort.

Your task, and that of the professional healers helping your loved one, is to participate in this ultimate faithful commitment. Indeed, reaching into this unknowing can be a source of great strength, and the mysterious source of your ability to facilitate growth and healing in the dying process. How do you do this? How do you act beyond your knowledge? Neither Rilke nor Byock give specific direction. Rilke says to "make yourself fierce, break in," and Byock says to "ask of Rilke's unknowing."

When you are confronted with the persistence of your loved one's suffering, you must delve deeply into a part of yourself that you don't know very well and ask what is to be done. You need to develop an element of surrender to the unknowing, so that you can allow yourself to become a vehicle for more profound knowledge. Go back to the reasons you love this person and then validate those reasons. Be at peace with yourself and your role for the dying one. If you are not at peace, then draw upon your deepest inner strengths and bury your mental clutter, so that your mind is cleared and every thought is unfettered. Concentrate on what your loved one needs. Byock says that this process is driven by selfless, loving intent.

Confronting continual suffering—your loved one's as well as your own—requires humility and great courage. Overcoming fear and gathering up courage to do what you must is a huge part of facing your unknowing. Plus, if you truly allow yourself to be fierce and break in, your own suffering can be alleviated.

You will be transformed by your loved one's suffering by permitting "the great grief cry" to happen to you. Be aware and recognize that neither of you is alone. Perhaps Rilke's challenge to family members and caregivers will enable us all to regain skills of loving that are both necessary and lost.

It is important that you be conscious of how and what you can and cannot do. Be excruciatingly honest with yourself. If you can't do what is necessary (as we described above), allow your loved one to be helped by someone else. This does not mean that what you *can* do is insignificant; it simply means that someone else may be better at taking the leap to accompany your loved one. He or she can take over where you have to stop. There is nothing wrong with that.

We have no doubt, however, that you can overcome your fears with strong and unconditional love. This is a practice and skill that can be developed. In the long run, it will not just assist your loved one, but also will enhance your own soul.

Bargaining

I would give everything I own,

Give up my life, my heart, my home,

I would give everything I own

Just to see you once again

Just to touch you once again

—*Bread*

Bargaining is the beginning of an ongoing dialogue between your loved one and God. At first he attempts, through prayers and promises, to influence the will of the universe and change the course of his illness. Bargaining emerges from an insight or epiphany that tells him there is something *big* out there. The bargainer is beginning to realize that there is an order to the universe, and perhaps a god of some kind, and a system of reciprocity in the world. Bargaining is a rudimentary approach to spirituality. But remember that it is, for some, the first approach ever taken.

It can take very subtle forms, such that it could go unrecognized. We remember when a beloved friend was diagnosed with AIDS. The next year, during a traineeship at the AIDS Office in San Francisco, somewhere in our hearts was a prayer that God would see our good works and would not come and take our friend. This was bargaining: offering up good deeds for the return of his health.

Like denial, bargaining is often criticized as a hindrance to effectively confronting and coping with the trauma. It is sometimes seen as a form of spiritual impoverishment. We think the bargaining phase of grief offers many gifts to your loved one and contributes enormously to the spiritual growth that needs to take place. You and your loved one will both undergo a bargaining process.

Bargaining can be the door which, when opened, leads to deeper spiritual understanding and growth. Even in its narrowest form, bargaining entails consideration for some spiritual concepts, perhaps long abandoned, and an increased desire for understanding. Bargaining is the vehicle by which your loved one comes to a more complete and integrated understanding of his place in the universe and his relationship to God. The gift of bargaining is connectedness.

Those—dying then

Knew where they went—

They went to God's right hand—

That hand is amputated now

And God cannot be found—

The abdication of belief

Makes behavior small

Better an ignis fatuus

Than no illume at all—

—*Emily Dickinson*

Whose Death Is It, Anyway?

Dr. Sherwin Nuland, a renowned palliative care physician, says, "People must now take back the end of life from doctors, just as they took back the beginning of life." Your participation in the end of life—and the actual death—of your loved one helps him reclaim ownership of himself.

During this time of prescription drugs, doctor appointments, and hospital visits, it's important to remember that death is not a medical event. It is a personal event. It belongs to the dying—no one else. It belongs to you and your dying loved one.

That said, there may be a power struggle between you, your loved one, and the medical caregivers. Although the disease, the pain, the right to refuse care, and the actual death ultimately belong to your loved one, those who tend to him are also emotionally invested. Given how doctors are educated, how they practice medicine and surgery, and the general milieu of medical care in the western world, allowing the dying one to keep control of his own destiny can challenge and test these professionals in many ways. Furthermore, the health-care professional's workload may be so overburdening that he or she doesn't have time or inclination to relinquish the control that he or she wants to assert. This is all the more reason for you, the loving friend or family member, to relinquish issues of control and to support the choices your loved one makes. You may not be able to control the behavior or time constraints of the doctor, but you do have power over your own. Be wise with it, and be diligent not to impose your own control on your loved one.

Remember that this is a time of unpredictable events and emotions. There will be times when you feel that the world is careening out of control and you can do nothing about it. Sometimes this is true. Rather than wasting your time and emotions on trying to control outside forces and events, the best advice we can give you is to take a deep breath and realize that this spinning world will eventually settle down. You don't have to be in total control all of the time. This may be a timely mechanism for you to give some control back to your loved one and allow him to be empowered over his death. In transferring some of your control to your loved one, you may also become more accepting of the losses you are experiencing—especially the death of someone you love.

The hospice movement in America has brought about a needed shift in the health-care industry. The focus has changed from trying to cure and treat disease (in the face of obvious failure) to alleviating pain and caring for the emotional and spiritual life of your loved one.

It is important to distinguish between pain and suffering. Pain is physical. It is the body's response to injury or disease. Suffering is subjective. It is a quality of the soul. It involves the way we experience pain and the meaning we assign to it. The pain a young boy feels when skidding on his knees into home plate is mingled with the cheers and applause of the crowd, and a feeling of excitement and success. If the umpire yells "Out!" the quality of that pain is altered, and suffering begins. Your loved one will have a similar experience with his pain. The quality of his end-of-life care, and the emotional comfort he takes in the love of his family and friends, will influence the extent and depth of his suffering, no matter the extent of the pain.

The relief of physical pain and the alleviation of suffering is a vital part of returning control to your loved one. There are many methods and medications for pain control. As disease progresses, dosages increase, and methods of delivery change. Many people have an intravenous pump system for delivery of pain medications. A constant dose of morphine or other pain medication is delivered intravenously as a steady drip. However, your dying loved has the control of a larger dose, if needed. A button can be pushed several times an hour (usually every five minutes); it delivers an extra measure of medication. The amount of medication has been pre-set for both the drip and bolus amounts to prevent overdose. We will talk more about pain control later.

Choosing Where to Die

Perhaps the most empowering choice you can leave to your loved one is that of where she would like to die. Most people want to die at home. You may have fears about her dying at home. Caring for a person at the end of her life can be daunting and can seem overwhelming. You may wonder if you are up to this task, physically and psychologically. If you decide you are not, consider that in most communities there is assistance available in the form of home-care services, home hospice agencies, and respite care.

When you get the prognosis that your loved one is within six months of dying, your physician may order hospice home care. Your hospice agency will provide a specialized interdisciplinary team consisting of a registered nurse, a medical social worker, a home health aide, a chaplain, and perhaps a volunteer from the community. You may or may not meet the physician or medical director who may manage the symptoms of your dying loved one's terminal illness, but your own doctor will still be there with you.

Following the referral from your doctor, a nurse or case manager will come to your home to meet with you and your loved one. The purpose of this meeting, known as an intake interview, is to provide you with information about end-of-life issues and to explain how hospice services can support everyone through the process. You'll be asked questions about your own beliefs, values, and wishes, as well as those of your loved one. This discussion will help you decide if the hospice philosophy and practice is consistent with your loved one's situation. Keep in mind that hospice provides palliative care. It is not appropriate for people who are pursuing curative treatments.

When someone is a hospice patient, the hospice agency becomes the care manager. All costs of managing the terminal illness are usually assumed by the hospice agency. Hospice provides medications related to the terminal condition, home nursing and social work visits, and home health aide visits to assist with bathing and hygiene, as the illness progresses. With very rare exceptions for the palliation of pain, hospice does not provide chemotherapy, radiation therapy, or surgery. Although hospice agencies deliver care in the home, most hospices do provide brief hospitalizations if needed for pain management and respite care, which can be delivered in a nursing home or an actual hospice house.

Hospice, like other home-care services, is intermittent care. As the disease progresses, visits increase in number and duration. However, your loved one must have a caregiver who can be with him twenty-four hours a day when needed. This can be a role that is shared among family and friends. You can also hire a trained caregiver privately or through an agency. Hospice caregivers are there to guide you and other caregivers through the process, and are available twenty-four hours a day, seven days a week.

When death is imminent, there may be someone to help you and your loved one through the dying process.

The Paperwork

At the initial visit, the nurse will ask if your loved one has an "advance directive" or a "durable power of attorney" for health care. This is a legal document specifying your loved one's choices regarding end-of-life care. It can also name an agent to act on his behalf if he should become unable to speak for himself. If you have such a document, she will ask you for a copy of these papers. If not, the hospice social worker can assist you in completing the forms.

Your loved one or his representative will also be asked to sign a "hospice waiver." In effect, this assigns your loved one's Medicare or other health-care insurance reimbursement to the hospice agency. In return, the hospice agency covers the expenses related to care. Most health-care policies (including Medicare, HMOs, Medicaid, and private insurance) have provisions for hospice home care. Non-profit hospice agencies are often supported financially by the community. Many hospice agencies have funds to provide special services and to extend care to uninsured and underinsured patients. Ask the caseworker assigned to you.

The Big Decisions

Many hospice agencies require that their patients have "do not resuscitate" (DNR) status. The patient and loved ones must agree that as death approaches, paramedics will not be called. Emergency or heroic measures will not be requested or allowed. Your loved one will be allowed to die in peace. You may be given a prominent "paramedic DNR" form to keep in your home. If paramedics are summoned, it is often presumed that the patient wants all efforts made to restore and maintain life. In fact, in many states it is law that the paramedics *cannot* decide to *not* resuscitate once they are called, regardless of any prior paperwork. When you call them they *will* resuscitate and transport a person to the nearest hospital emergency room. The paramedic DNR form *may* clarify your wishes and prevent unwanted attempts at cardiopulmonary resuscitation.

You will have a folder with the names of your hospice team members, their phone numbers, and any instructions or information you will need in order to maintain a relationship with the hospice team. Often you will also be given stickers printed with the hospice phone number to put on your telephones. This is a visual reminder to call the hospice agency in an emergency and *not* to call 911. There will be a hospice nurse on duty twenty-four hours a day to help you and your loved one through this. They will be there for you.

The Hospice Team

The hospice team holds weekly case conferences, and its members consult among themselves often about the care of every patient and family member. If you have any specific concerns and issues with the entire team, you may be able to participate in this process, so that all issues surrounding your loved one's death can be addressed.

Your case manager is a registered nurse with special training and experience in both home care and terminal care. She will visit regularly to monitor your loved one's condition. She will consult with your doctor or the hospice physician to provide effective pain control and symptom management. She will instruct the family on the administration of this medication. She will also serve to coordinate the rest of your care with the team, to ensure that care is comprehensive and responsive to your changing needs.

The hospice social worker has a master's degree in social work and is often a licensed mental-health practitioner. She will help you with the emotional, psychological, and logistic issues you are now facing. She can also assist in expediting much of the overwhelming paperwork and details associated with dying. She can help identify and access community resources. She can answer questions about final arrangements for the body. You will see her often, and you will come to know each other well.

The hospice chaplain is interdenominational. She is not there to sell you on a religion. She is with you to assist you in connecting with your own spiritual values and beliefs. She can provide linkage to a minister, priest, or rabbi of your own denomination, if you wish. She is available to provide support and witness to your journey as often or as little as you desire.

If needed, a home health aide can visit up to several times a week to help with bathing, changing sheets, feeding, and providing personal care. No matter what your physical condition, you will be treated with compassion, kindness, and respect. No one is kinder, gentler, or more loving than a hospice home health aide.

Often people need the help of physical therapists to recover lost function or maintain maximum strength. The strength to walk to the kitchen table is worth preserving. The stamina to sit in a favorite chair and visit a favorite grandchild lends grace and meaning to life. Hospice can send a physical therapist as needed so that all potential functions can be maintained.

When someone you love is dying, it may seem like the world has stopped spinning—like nothing else is going on. This is an illusion that will soon be shattered.

There are still appointments to keep, errands to run, and shopping that must be done. Many families are far-flung across the globe. Friends work and commute long distances. This is where the hospice volunteer can make all the difference. A hospice volunteer is a member of your community. He is there because he wants to be there. He has undergone a great deal of training about end-of-life issues, grief, and bereavement. This person can stay with your loved one while you leave the house for an hour or two, or while you stay at home and have a nap.

Institutional Care

For some people, dying at home is not an option. If your own health is frail, you will not be able to care for a dying person. Or, for example, if your dying father is a widower and you need to work or care for young children in your own home, you will not be able to provide round-the-clock terminal care in his home. Families are smaller and geographically separated, and economic realities often necessitate that both partners work outside the home. A loving daughter in Boston may insist, "I want my father to die at home in his own bed in San Diego." But does she know if she can really be there at the moment of death? And what of her eighty-six-year-old mother? Can this elderly woman feed, bathe, and diaper a dying man? Can she sit at his bedside hour after hour when he falls into a coma? Can she listen to his breath become labored without having care and support for herself?

If the patient's physical needs are great and the capacity to provide physical care is limited, the best choice for the comfort of the patient and the family is terminal care at a skilled nursing facility, hospital, or hospice house.

Many people do not live in separate private homes in the last years of their lives. If your loved one is extremely frail and perhaps suffers from some form of senile dementia, he may already live in a residential-care facility. Placing a loved one into any facility brings with it an acknowledgment that death is occurring. Your father, husband, lover, uncle, or dear friend can no longer maintain his independence at home. His frailty, dementia, incontinence, or some cruel mix of all these symptoms has robbed him of a cherished part of who he is.

Residential-care facilities are sometimes small enterprises. They resemble other homes in the neighborhood. They provide round-the-clock staff to help residents with dressing and grooming. They provide all meals and snacks, and assistance with medication management. They are licensed, usually by the state's board of health and human services. If your loved one's normal residence is an assisted-living facility or a residential-care home, hospice home services can often be delivered to that facility. The facility is the caregiver, and the patient's medical insurance (usually Medicare) reimburses hospice for end-of-life services.

Residents of skilled nursing homes who are living there on a private-pay basis or under long-term care reimbursement through a Medicaid program are often able to utilize their Medicare or senior HMO benefits to have hospice care. The patient remains at the nursing home. The nursing home is the twenty-four-hour caregiver. However, the hospice team comes in and manages the loved one's terminal comfort care. Alternately, this may be available at the skilled nursing facility through staff members who offer hospice care.

The residential caregivers have joined you as a part of your peripheral family, and all is still the same. The "home" has only changed, and there are more caregivers for your loved one.

Whether your loved one is facing imminent death or going into a long and dwindling season of sunsets, finding a caring and supportive environment for him is an act of love.

Death in a Hospital

If pain is very bad, exacerbation of symptoms occurs, or more structured support is needed, your loved one may spend his final days in a hospital. As medicine has advanced, even the normal and natural events of birth and death often occur in a hospital. This setting may feel unfamiliar and very uncomfortable to your family and dying loved one. As a caregiver, you may feel that your role has been reduced to being a mere spectator rather than a necessary and vital part of your loved one's life and a key figure in this transition. The nurses and technicians may seem to know everything, to do everything, and to make the majority of the decisions. In this setting, the family often feels marginalized. This institutionalized setting can be challenging and intimidating.

Tips for Positive Hospital Experiences

Hospitals are getting better at supporting families and dying people through their deaths. There are many things you can do to assure that your loved one's needs for dignity, peace, and wholeness will be honored and supported. For starters, let the hospital staff know your wishes and those of your loved one.

- Be prepared. Be clear. Be specific. Let your loved one's nurse know what treatments and therapies he wants and doesn't want. This covers much more than simple ventilator support. You will want to discuss other forms of life support, including artificial hydration and nutrition, kidney dialysis, intravenous antibiotics, medications such as dopamine that artificially maintain blood pressure, and internal pace makers that do not allow a heart to stop beating.

- If there is an advance directive or durable power of attorney for health care, bring the document with you to the hospital and ask that it be included in his medical chart.

- Be certain that everyone knows and understands his wishes about CPR.

- Request that DNR be prominently marked on the front of the medical chart.

- You can sometimes adjust the hospital environment, making it feel more like home. Bring family photos into the room. Replace blank hospital walls with artwork your loved one likes. If you are discouraged by hospital staff, speak with the head nurse so that some welcome changes may be effected. Sometimes small items that your loved has enjoyed can be provided in his room. These may include favorite foods or drinks, movies, a piece of work that needs to be finished, a family scrapbook, music, or perhaps old letters. Sometimes a family pet may offer peace.

Many hospitals have palliative care units, or skilled nursing units where you and your dying loved one can be more comfortably accommodated. These areas of the hospital are accustomed to dealing with people who are dying. The staff is often calmer, more experienced, more supportive of the dying process, and better able to provide sensitive end-of-life support. These units have more flexible visitor schedules as well. In general, children are more likely to be welcome in non-acute areas of the hospital and are given more support and attention throughout the process. Let the staff know that there are many family members and friends who will be visiting.

We hope that by raising this particularly nettlesome dynamic, it will serve to educate everyone so you can work together as a team to allow your loved one to own his death. Again, this is the true test of caregivers of all kinds, including you, and the last opportunity to do what you can for your terminally ill loved one. Your loved one wants to die with your consent and your blessing. How this consent is given is of the utmost importance, and you may not even notice doing it! We will share those clues and ways to listen for this in a later chapter.

4

THANKSGIVING: ACKNOWLEDGING THE BOUNTY OF LIFE

The third week of November seems like an odd time to give thanks. Autumn has advanced like a conquering infantry, leaving the world crisp and dry and still. Even the most hopeful leaf has abandoned the tree and lies lifeless on the lawn. The brisk fall air that seemed so refreshing in early October is colder and heavier. It gnaws on the bones. September, the month of the first chill, seems light-years away. And the rowdiness of summer, if remembered at all, feels like a dream of another place, another life. Ushered in by Labor Day and punctuated by Halloween and El Dia de los Muertos (The Day of the Dead), this is indeed an odd time to be thankful.

Yet this cusp-of-winter holiday elicits our thankfulness and brings forth our love for each other. It evokes our generosity. It reminds us of how good and loving we can be. The containers for canned food sprout up in front of grocery stores and are filled quickly. People volunteer to serve Thanksgiving dinner at soup kitchens and homeless shelters. No one should be hungry now. No one should be cold. No one should be alone. No one should be ill or dying.

This holiday has no bright lights. There are no presents. There are no Thanksgiving pageants at Rockefeller Center (or at the grammar school). There are no songs or particular music associated with it. In the final journey of our lives, there is also a time to remember who we are and to acknowledge the bounty of life. There is a metaphoric Thanksgiving. As in real time, it occurs after the first frosts—after the malaise, after the diagnosis, after the second opinion. After the first shocks of a life-threatening illness, after the denial and the depression, after the beginning of the unending cadence of losses. After El Dia de los Muertos. After the beginning of life review. After the beginning of grieving.

Somewhere in all of this, hope emerges. Real hope. The poet Havel defines hope this way: "Hope is a quality of the spirit. It is not the belief that things will turn out well, but the knowledge that things will make sense, however they turn out."

This time of reflection, of reconnecting, of remembering will usher in the "winter lights." Winter lights are the epiphanies and the miracles of the soul that will provide light and warmth against the coming darkness. It is early in the seasons. The work of dying for you and your loved one has barely begun. The story of Irene that follows shows how a dying loved one can find hope at the end of life through the spirit of thanksgiving, even if one was not present before.

Irene

Irene was one of those patients nurses complain about to each other. At a change of shift, they will sometimes trade two "regular" patients for one "Irene."

She had never enjoyed good health. Irene had suffered from a variety of chronic illnesses, including diabetes, asthma, and arthritis. She had married briefly in her younger days and had two children, now adults, and several grandchildren. She lived alone in a small mobile home in the country.

Irene was a frequent patient at the hospital and in the health clinics. It seemed she was always being treated for some minor infection or the repercussions of one of her chronic illnesses. Irene had a sorrowful, almost mournful personality, and she had many complaints about her health and the lack of solicitude of her family and medical-care team. "Can't they see how sick I am?" she would ask. "Doesn't anyone give a damn about me?"

One of the saddest parts of this story is that Irene's constant fixation on her physical discomforts and her complaining about family and caregivers had, in fact, caused her to be alienated and very much alone. Her call light really did get answered last. Her room really was at the end of the hall. Her doctor really did conduct his bedside visits from the hallway. Irene was a very unhappy woman in a very unhappy situation.

Irene had been complaining of belly pain for months, and tests were run which turned up nothing. Her complaints persisted. She was given a variety of medications, sent to biofeedback training, and finally dismissed as simply being neurotic. Then there was a diagnosis.

Irene had stomach cancer that had spread to her pancreas and liver. The metastasis was far too widespread to be treated. Irene was going to die.

We had visited Irene many times during her multiple hospitalizations, and Pam particularly dreaded this visit. One of the nurses had said of her, "It's like she plugs a vacuum-cleaner hose into your heart and sucks the life out of you."

As we approached Irene's room, something felt different...it felt somehow lighter. We looked in and saw Irene busy at her handiwork. Irene was a jewelry maker, selling her wares at country fairs and art festivals throughout Northern California. She was propped up in her bed, so absorbed in her work that she didn't notice us at first.

"Hello, Irene," Pam said from the doorway, "how are you feeling?" In retrospect, we were afraid of the answer. She looked up at us over the rim of her glasses and smiled.

"Not bad…considering." Then she beckoned us in. We took chairs next to her bed, and Pam took her hand.

"Irene," Pam told her, "you are not going to be able to go home. There's nobody there to take care of you, and you are very sick."

She told Irene that her doctor had ordered her to be transferred to Hospice House the following day. The window in Irene's room was open, and a cold wind blew in, scattering some of the small sequins and beads she was working with. Pam got up and attempted to retrieve all of them from the floor. Irene laughed. It was the first time we had ever heard her laugh. It was beautiful.

"I'm way ahead of you," she said. "It's real this time, isn't it? I'm going to die?"

Pam nodded. "But the doctor says you have time."

Irene shook her head. "When is Thanksgiving?" she asked. Pam told her that Thanksgiving was in two days, and that she would have time and health to celebrate Thanksgiving and Christmas. Irene stopped her.

"I have Thanksgiving," she said, "and I will celebrate for probably the first time in my life. I will celebrate my life and my children. I will celebrate being here. Then I am gone."

We looked at her, puzzled.

"I have believed in sickness all my life," she explained. "Now I will believe in my life. And when my life is over, I am not going to hold onto this beat-up body for an extra minute. I will be gone."

Before the ambulance came to take Irene to Hospice House, she took Pam's hand and placed a pair of earrings in her palm. "These are for you, my good friend," she said. "There's aventurine in these. Remember to appreciate the adventure."

And then Irene's gurney disappeared behind the elevator doors.

On Thanksgiving Day, Irene's doctor and his family were at Pam's home. They were all sitting around the table chatting when his pager went off. He took the call in another room. He returned to the table looking white and shocked. "That was Hospice House," he said. "Irene's kids came to Thanksgiving dinner with her. They ate, the kids left, and Irene went to her room and died."

Death can provide resolution for the incongruities of life, as it did for Irene. Death can be a source of hope that wholeness and love can manifest at any moment along our journey, and that it is always *just in time*.

Managing Pain and Nausea

Pain is a complicated dynamic. It is affected by our emotional health, our surroundings, our culture, and our age. Children, for instance, feel and respond to pain much more acutely than do adults. And some people, for reasons we do not fully understand, are more sensitive to pain than other people. They just hurt more than other people, given the same stimulus.

Keep in mind that there is *always* something that can be done for pain. The American Cancer Society and National Institutes of Health offer excellent publications on pain relief that will help prepare you and your loved one for what's to come.

If your loved one is in pain, you need to consult with the doctor about the best approach to managing it. Once you have the steps necessary to do that, you should know certain things about pain. Ask the following questions of your loved one:

- Do you have pain? (This is not asked often enough.)
- Where is the pain?
- On a scale of one to ten, can you tell me how much it hurts?
- What is its character? Is it dull, sharp, intermittent?
- Does it get worse, or stay the same?
- Does it stay in one spot, or does it radiate?
- Does it help to change position, or is the pain exacerbated by movement?
- What makes it better?
- What makes it worse?
- Would you like medication for your pain?

Be mindful that pain is often accompanied by nausea, dizziness, weakness, constipation, dry mouth, inability to void, insomnia, loss of appetite, fear, anger, crying, depression, suicidal thoughts, and verbal abuse of you. In view of this, it's vitally important that you and your loved one understand the nature of pain and the most effective and timely ways in which you can respond.

After your doctor evaluates the overall condition, strength, and nature of pain being experienced by your loved one, and considering the impact of the accompanying symptoms, he or she will most likely order, suggest, or prescribe:

- pharmacological (drug) relief
- nerve blocks
- radiation therapy
- distraction
- guided imagery
- breathing exercises
- self-hypnosis
- repositioning
- hot/cold compresses
- ice pack
- heating pad
- light massage
- Reiki
- acupuncture
- acupressure

Pharmacological and Common Medical Definitions

Don't be intimidated by medical jargon. These terms are only a part of the language that you, as a partner in the care of your loved one, will come to learn and understand quickly.

Addiction: Psychological, physical, or emotional dependence on the effects of a drug.

Analgesic: Medication used to treat pain.

Anesthesiologist: A doctor who is a specialist in pain control.

Antidepressant: Medication that is used to treat depression or elevate mood. Commonly prescribed antidepressants include Prozac, Wellbutrin, and Paxil.

Anti-emetic: A medication to treat nausea. May cause drowsiness.

Carcinoma: Medical term for cancer of the epithelial tissue. (This is the layer of cells that covers other tissues and structures)

Chemotherapy: Cancer treatment by drugs.

Dose: An amount of drug or medicine that is given.

Emesis: Vomiting; nausea.

Epidural: An injection into the layers of body tissue around the spinal cord.

Infusion: A way to deliver the drug into a vein or under the skin by needle.

IM: Intramuscular. An injection delivered into the muscle.

IV: Intravenous. An injection delivered into the vein.

Lymphoma: A malignant cancer of the lymph system.

Melanoma: A malignant cancer of the skin.

Metastasis: Spreading of cancer or tumor from one site to another in the body. Metastasis can be local (spreading to the next organ in the body) or distant (occurring in more remote parts of the body).

Narcotic: A class of pain medication derived from opium. Narcotics are very helpful in the treatment of moderate to severe pain.

Neoplasm: Another medical word for cancer.

Nerve block: A way to block pain from traveling down a nerve.

PCA pump: Patient-controlled analgesic. An IV that delivers a consistent amount of pain medication. The patient can self-administer additional medication by pushing a button. The levels are set to prevent accidental overdose.

Side effect: An unintended symptom from a drug.

Staging: A method of gauging the spread of cancer.

Subcutaneous: Delivering a drug under the skin.

Sublingual: Beneath the tongue. Often a liquid form of morphine is given in drops administered below the tongue. You can also place a couple of drops between the lower teeth and the cheek.

While we are primarily addressing the pharmacology of physical pain, there are other types of pain that will also inflict a burden on your dying loved one. They include spiritual, emotional, and social pain.

From Over-the-Counter Drugs to Prescription Pharmaceutical Relief

As disease progresses and death approaches, medications may become the first line of defense against pain and anxiety. Other modalities, such as hypnotism and guided imagery, lose their effectiveness because your loved one may not be able to concentrate or follow instructions anymore. All medications have some side effects. Pain medications in particular have side effects like constipation, sleepiness, or compromised mental acuity. Sleepiness will often subside as your loved one's body adjusts to the medication. These side effects may recur when the dose of the medication is increased, but will likely again subside.

Once everyone agrees that administering drugs is the most appropriate choice for managing pain, the doctor will probably start with over-the-counter medications such as acetaminophen (Tylenol) or aspirin. If these are not effective, non-steroidal anti-inflammatory medications (NSAIDS) such as Advil and Motrin—both brand names for ibuprofen—will likely be prescribed. Some common side effects of NSAIDS include upset stomach and nausea. Stomach bleeding occurs on rare occasions. Check with your doctor or pharmacist to ascertain whether there could be interactions with other drugs your loved one may be taking.

Easing Stomach Discomfort

Sometimes aspirin or ibuprofen can cause an upset tummy. Who needs that on top of everything else? One simple solution is to take the aspirin or ibuprofen with food. It may take a bit longer for them to work, but most people are happy with the trade-off.

Be mindful that all drugs wear off after a certain amount of time, and that your loved one will want more relief as soon as possible. Don't overdo it. Never administer more than a total of ten to twelve adult-size (325 mg) aspirins or acetaminophen pills (Tylenol) in a twenty-four-hour period. Watch the time, too. Refrain from giving more than seven or eight 500-mg tablets.

If over-the-counter drugs are not effective in reducing the pain, it is time to move on to prescription medications. Don't run out—it may be difficult to get refills on a holiday weekend or after hours.

Aspirin, acetaminophen, and ibuprofen come in combination with codeine or other narcotics. They may be used alone, or in combination with over-the-counter medications. Some familiar names include:

- Aspirin or tylenol with codeine
- Vicodin
- Lorcet
- Lortab
- Norco
- Vicoprofen
- Percodan
- Percocet
- Darvon
- Darvocet N

Other common drugs, known as narcotics or opioids (because they are derived from opium) will fill your medicine cabinets and bedside tables. If children are around, however, be sure to keep all of these drugs in a safe place. Use these medications only as directed. The narcotics you may become familiar with include:

- Codeine (plain, not in combination)
- Morphine
- Oxycodone
- Methadone
- Hydromorphone (Dilaudid)
- Oxymorphone (Numorphan)

Morphine comes in all sorts of varieties and is the most commonly used pain medication. It is available in long-acting (twenty-four-hour) or short-acting doses. Morphine is available in tablet, capsule, liquid, and intravenous forms.

Addiction to narcotics is a common concern among people who need them. Many studies have shown, however, that patients who are in pain do not become addicted to pain-relieving medications if they discontinue the use of these drugs once the pain is resolved. In the setting of a terminal condition, concerns about addiction are simply not relevant.

Another phenomenon that may happen is drug tolerance. Medication dosages must often be increased as disease progresses. This is a natural and expected occurrence. Again, with terminal illnesses, this need not be the subject of concern.

Side effects occur with some regularity. The most common side effects are sleepiness and constipation. Sleepiness often resolves as the body adjusts to medication. Even so, there is always going to be a dance between pain control and alertness. Constipation, on the other hand, can be treated with laxatives and stool softeners.

It is important to report your concerns about side effects or changes in the condition of your loved one to the physician or hospice team. Dangerous drug interactions, or contraindications, can and do occur with narcotics. Alcohol, sleeping medications, tranquilizers, and over-the-counter medications such as antihistamines used for colds and congestion can all cause problems. Be sure that your prescribing physician is aware of all the other medications your loved one is taking. Don't forget herbal supplements as they, too, can either interfere with the drugs or cause side effects.

If your loved one is experiencing nausea and vomiting, you need to get to the root of what's causing it. If it is from the pain, it will go away with pain control. If it is from cancer spread to the brain or bowel obstruction, then your doctor or hospice team will need to get stronger anti-nausea medicine for you. This may include Compazine, Tigan, or Torecan. These will also work for the nausea and vomiting from side effects from other medications.

Antidepressants, such as Elavil (which can also help nerve pain) and some of the newer antidepressant drugs (Celexa, Prozac, Zoloft), may also be used to help manage pain—or depression from having to cope with the condition. Anticonvulsant drugs and steroids may help in reducing seizures or pressure on nerves by tumors, which may also cause sleepiness, nausea and vomiting or pain.

As you negotiate how to relieve your loved one's pain, you may also consider using complementary methods: relaxation techniques, biofeedback, guided imagery, hypnotism, distraction, skin stimulation, TENS units, massage, pressure points, acupuncture, and vibration. Bookstores are filled with information on these modalities, or you can ask the hospice team or your physician what they recommend. Don't be afraid to experiment with any of these techniques—they work quite well with many types of pain.

The extra benefit of many of these techniques is that they don't simply relieve pain, they give comfort and pleasure, and they convey your love.

References and Readings

Bolen, Jean Shinoda, MD, <u>The Tao of Psychology: Synchronicity and the Self</u>, Harper and Row, 1982.

Siegel, Bernie, MD, <u>Love, Medicine and Miracles</u>, Harper and Row, 1988.

Meier, Diane E, "Opinion: A Change of Heart on Assisted Suicide," *New York Times,* April 24, 1998.

Harris, J. et al., "The Importance of the Doctor to the Dying Patient," *Southern Medical Journal,* October 1979, Vol. 72, No. 10, pp. 1319-25.

Nuland, Sherwin B., in "How We Die: Reflections on Life's Final Chapters," Knopf, New York, 1994.

5

DECEMBER: WINTER LIGHTS

O holy night

The stars are brightly shining

In the middle of every winter there is a festival of light and warmth, and so it is with the soul's winter: the soul of your dying loved one. The festival tides us over through the cold and darkness, and provides the lamp with which we can see our way. Similarly, in the journey toward death, which often feels dark and cold and frightening, there are periods of light and warmth. These are truly times of healing and joy. Our allusion to the winter festivals of light is metaphoric for your experience of this healing.

The metaphoric December is the pivotal month in your loved one's transition from life to death. It is the time of deep spiritual insight and connection to one's own definition of holiness. We are reminded in December that life is not contained by us—we are contained by life. The soul's winter is the time when your loved one's hope for life transforms to a hope and desire for a comfortable transition into the next realm. This hope is attached to a broader meaning of life, and transfers easily to a more global perspective of existence. The season of lights serves to restore the love and sense of well-being and thankfulness that will guide this transformation.

Changes in Relationships

Relationships once distant can be transformed as people put down truly petty and insignificant differences. Other relationships, ones that were always more window-dressing than personal, can now be explored in light of the impending transition from life to death. Sometimes these relationships can be reclaimed and their meanings woven into the context of one's personal story and experience. Other times, simply acknowledging the human emotions and limitations in this near-final season can free one to invest in relationships and activities that have deeper meaning and bring a sense of wholeness and joy. And of course, there are miracles. The December of the soul is also about miracles.

It is important to remember that not all miracles happen before our eyes. They often occur within our hearts and are heard only by our souls.

Sharon's Nova

Sharon was thirteen when Pam met her. She was willowy and beautiful with waist-length black hair and sparkling eyes. She had been raised most of her life by her grandmother in the Philippines. Her parents had been here for over ten years, working twelve-hour days in the hospitality industry of Monterey to earn enough money to establish a home and to send for their beloved daughter. America was still very new to Sharon. She was somewhat timid, sometimes looking awkwardly into her lap during conversations. And this was going to be a very difficult conversation.

Sharon's oncologist had phoned Pam that afternoon and asked her to join him at the family conference to discuss one of his patients. "She's a kid," he said.

"Is it bad?" Pam asked. The phone was silent for a moment. Then he replied, "She will die of this."

And so, in an antiseptic little room, the doctor explained that Sharon's tumor was very rare and that there was no treatment available locally. He said that she might qualify for a clinical study in UCSF. He would look into it.

"What does all this mean?" asked Sharon's mother, looking from face to face for reassurance that just wasn't forthcoming.

The doctor cleared his throat. "This is very bad," he said, "and it is very advanced. I will look into the clinical studies for you in the morning."

All this time, Sharon sat silently, staring into her lap. Finally, she spoke.

"School is starting in a couple of weeks. I'm going into junior high." She paused, twisting a strand of her shiny black hair. "Am I going to lose my hair?"

The doctor looked at her and nodded, adding, "It'll grow back." And Sharon sank back into silence.

Sharon's family took her to see the specialists at UCSF. She underwent an aggressive chemotherapy regime. Pam didn't see her again until the cusp of winter, a grim and wet late November afternoon, when Sharon was brought to the fifth floor in a wheelchair. Sharon's treatment had resulted in her "going neutropenic." She had no more immune system or white blood cells to fight infection and would need to be admitted for reverse isolation to prevent infection.

It was the first of many admissions that winter. Pam hardly recognized Sharon that afternoon. Her slender body was all bones and taut gray skin. Her face, always placid, was staring blankly ahead. On her head she wore a too-large turban. Sharon was ravaged and looked old.

Although Sharon didn't have many friendships among her peers, she was the centerpiece of her family's existence. They belonged to a large and supportive church family that held special services and prayer vigils for her recovery.

Sharon's caregivers at the hospital loved her. They guarded her as best they could from pain and discomfort. Her doctor was especially devoted and tender with her. He had a talent for impersonating celebrities that few people knew about. He would do his impressions for Sharon just to see her smile. When he did Elvis, she laughed.

Sharon was an artist. She could draw or paint the things she couldn't say with words. The art therapist worked with Sharon whenever she was in the hospital. She was a cancer survivor herself, so she and Sharon shared a special bond. At Christmas time, Sharon and several other teens that were in the hospital created ornaments for the hospital Christmas tree. They spent a rainy Saturday with papier-mâché and white paste, getting glitter all over their hands and faces. Sharon worked quietly on her ornaments. Sometimes Pam would wander over to her and try to engage her in conversation. Sharon would smile and respond politely, but inevitably she would end up staring into her lap.

We were starting a new support group for teens with cancer at the hospital. We wanted it to be more age-appropriate than the normal support group, with an emphasis on activities and on normalizing the experience of cancer treatment.

Pam encouraged Sharon go on a trip to the Monterey Bay Aquarium. It was early spring, and the world was hopeful and new. Sharon participated in the outing. It may have been more to please Pam than to fill a need she had. She didn't socialize with the others teenagers; she held herself apart. When everyone stopped briefly to sit on the benches and watch the sea otters play, Sharon was staring into her lap—or maybe she was staring into her heart, at the truth. She was dying. She did not want to socialize with the other kids. She was distancing herself from the world. She was gathering the strength and the courage she would need to leave the family that adored her and the people she loved most, to journey into the unknown.

One afternoon in early summer, Sharon was in the hospital for a blood transfusion. Pam was sitting on her bed. This time, both of them were staring into their laps. Finally, Sharon spoke.

"You know, Pam, I think about lots of things. I mean…there's lots going on inside my mind. I just don't talk about it a lot. But I know I won't live long."

"What kinds of things do you think about? Can you tell me about them?"

"I don't think so," she replied, "I just don't think so."

There was an uncomfortable silence for a few minutes. Then Sharon asked if the art therapist was around. She had left, but Pam offered to get the art supplies for Sharon, who gratefully accepted. Pam got the supplies, gave her a quick hug, and left for the day, figuring that perhaps Sharon didn't want to talk that day.

The next morning, there was a huge picture on Pam's desk. It was Sharon's profile: her quiet, passive face staring into the future. But inside the head were colors and shapes and starbursts and an aliveness that defied death. On the picture was a yellow sticky tab, on which she had written: "To Pam—Thanks for everything. Love, Sharon."

Pam never saw Sharon again. The evening she did the drawing, she went home, and she died a couple of weeks later, surrounded by her family. They reported that she had died peacefully and quietly—in just the way she had lived. And yet her picture says so much: an exploding nova, speaking of movement and excitement, of discovery and growth and joy. Sharon's aliveness was within her. Her picture is now framed and hangs on Pam's wall.

Sharon taught us that living, loving, and communicating are properties of the spirit as well as the senses. Sometimes we have to listen, not just with our ears, but with our eyes, our minds and our hearts. Your loved one may speak in symbols, in pictures or in glances and sighs. If you listen with all that you are, perhaps she can help you heal a little part of yourself.

The Final Tasks of Life

Death has been called the final stage of growth. The potential for resolution and completion at the end of life is compelling. There is work to be done in the dying process. It is work that will give meaning, clarity, and a theme to one's life—work that will transform your loved one's death into something more significant than an ending. A life well-lived and completed is a reason to celebrate, and it is a lasting blessing for those whose love has helped. The final season of life is the time to bring seemingly unrelated fragments of experience together into a harmonious whole. It is a time for resolution and reconciliation.

It is important to remember that these events don't happen in random or linear ways. It is all going on at the same time.

The final tasks of life include the completion of the developmental tasks that teach us how to trust, how to grow as a person, how to be self-reliant, and how to say good-bye. Completion of these tasks is facilitated by life review, search for meaning and authenticity, and acceptance and acknowledgment.

In an address given to a local hospice organization, Dr. Byock stated that there are really only five things we must learn to say to each other to complete our journeys and our relationships together:

- "Forgive me."
- "I forgive you."
- "Thank you."
- "I love you."
- "Good-bye."

Perhaps in those brief words dwells the world's store of wisdom and love. Transforming those words into tangible actions and allowing the concepts to transform your own and your loved one's life can be the hard part. Use the following as guidelines:

- **"Forgive me."** Every couple, every family, and every loving relationship must weather difficult times: times of pain and misunderstanding; miscommunication, or no communication at all. Feelings are hurt, and there is resentment. Your loved one may be haunted by sharp words he said in a moment of anger. He may feel great guilt about his business and inattention to children or family during earlier years of the marriage. "Forgive me" may come in many different forms: "I wish I'd gone to Jenny's piano recital when she was a child," or "I never saw Jacob play baseball. I regret that."

We most often regret those things we did not do: the missed opportunities for closeness with loved ones. There is sadness that our presence and love was not felt at important life events.

Your loved one may also have deeply held regrets about things he did. These can range from acts of deceit and betrayal to simple moments of impatience and unkind words.

If your loved one expresses feelings of guilt, don't minimize them. Be present. Listen. It's okay to acknowledge imperfections in your relationship.

- **"I forgive you."** Giving your forgiveness does not imply that there was no pain or that you approve or condone past behavior that caused you pain. Forgiving means that you are laying down the burdens of anger and resentment.

Caroline Myss, PhD, is a medical intuitive who was instrumental in the Harvard research on complementary medicine. She has written eloquently about forgiveness in her books, including "Why People Don't Heal and How You Can." She speaks compellingly of the importance of forgiveness:

> Forgiveness is a complex act of consciousness, one that liberates the psyche and soul from the need for personal vengeance and the perception of oneself as a victim. More than releasing from blame the people who caused our wounds, forgiveness means releasing the control that the perception of victimization has over our psyches.

- Forgiveness needs to be conscious. It needs to be expressed. And sometimes it needs to be repeated. "I forgive you." You and your loved one both need to forgive.

- **"Thank you."** Sometimes the things that made us the happiest, or the ones that made the biggest difference in our lives, were seemingly small things: when he met your plane with flowers in his hands; when she massaged your feet after that long walk on cobblestones. These are not gestures that get letters of commendation or recognition from hordes of people, yet the quality of life is colored by these small and powerful moments. This is the time to acknowledge and express gratitude for the many small miracles of love you have shared with each other. "I remember that time…" "Did I ever tell you how much it meant to me when you…"

This is the time to say thank you.

- **"I love you."** As in: I love all of you, everything about you. But what do you love distinctly and passionately? Do you love his voice? Do you love her laugh? What are the specific things that you love, and in what specific ways do you love? Remember the poems from high school? The romantic poets? They were sentimental and elicited a certain quality from your heart. The poems seemed to be right on course:

How do I love thee? Let me count the ways.

I love thee to the depth and breadth and height

My soul can reach, when feeling out of sight

For the ends of being and ideal Grace.

I love thee to the level of everyday's

Most quiet need, by sun and candle-light.

I love thee freely, as men strive for Right.

I love thee purely, as they turn from Praise.

I love thee with the passion put to use

In my old grief, and with my childhood's faith.

I love thee with a love I seemed to lose

With my lost saints,—I love thee with the breath,

Smiles, tears, of my whole life!—and, if God choose,

I shall but love thee better after death.

—*Elizabeth Barrett Browning*

- **"Good-bye."** Saying good-bye is difficult. It can be done before or after the loved family member has died. You may have already begun this process. Your good-bye can be simple as just using the words above and a final hug or kiss, or it can be long and filled with statements of love and appreciation. The good-bye process can be a beginning of resolution for you. It will precede springtime as surely as day follows night. It heralds your readiness to begin a new life. You may have shared information with your loved one about your hopes and dreams for your continuing life. You may be going on to school, or taking a vacation with a beloved grandchild. Your loved one may have wishes of his own for you. It could be something as grand as wanting you to marry again, or something as simple as wanting you to wear a particular favorite dress to his funeral. This exchange of wishes for the future is a part of the good-bye process that leads to completion and resolution. There is potential for dynamic changes in what you once thought of as the rest of your life. Perhaps you need to have some time to resolve your grief. Perhaps you are ready to move on. Whatever your choice or need, rest assured you deserve your springtime—you have earned it. These thoughts at this time will enable you to face *the moment* when death actually occurs. You still have work to do. The festival of lights is the time to think of these things, and to begin your good-byes.

Achieving Resolution

Some circumstances cannot be resolved directly with your loved one. Sometimes relationships are too stressful, or your loved one is simply not able to participate in the process. Sometimes you have to come to your own resolution.

If your loved one has died, or if he cannot participate in conversations to resolve and heal your relationship, you may find solace talking to a priest, rabbi, or minister. Often just venting your feelings is helpful.

You can also try this meditation exercise to help address the issues of mending your heart. It may be difficult to do if you have not meditated before. Give it a try anyway: you might like it. We offer this because some of our patients have successfully come to resolution from practicing it. If this feels too foreign to you, pass it up and go on to the next section.

Exercise

Sit quietly in a comfortable position. Uncross your arms and legs. Become aware of your breathing. Breathe in deeply through your nose. Release the breath through your mouth. Follow your breath from your nostrils to your belly. Follow your breath seven times from your nostrils to your belly.

Concentrate on the weight in your lower abdomen and buttocks. Feel the heaviness there on the chair or cushion. Now draw your breath all the way from your nostrils above your upper lip…feel the temperature…down to the base of your spine. Draw your breath down the front of your spine, release it up the back of your spine, and then release it through your mouth.

Notice the changes in the temperature of your breath as it travels down your spine toward your center. Notice the feeling of the in-breath, the pause between breaths, and the feeling of the release. Follow your breath down your spine and up; do it seven times.

Next, imagine a shaft of energy traveling from the base of your spine down into the cushion that supports you. Follow the energy down from your body. Now go further, down into the earth. Go past the grass, the cool soil, and the grassy roots, past the clay and the small stones. Reach even deeper into a darker, warmer earth. Go down to the center of the world. Now, find something there to anchor your energy to. Find a tree or a rock or a post. Anchor your energy firmly to that. Then travel back up the trail, through the earth, back up to your body. Go back to your body and notice how firmly it is anchored to the center of the earth. You are unshakeable.

Next, follow your energy to the place between your eyes. Breathe. Follow your breath seven times to the base of your spine and out again. Get a sense of the person you want to address. Perhaps you can visualize him. Make the image as real and concrete as you can. Feel the presence of this person. Allow the scent of him to enter your consciousness. Breathe slowly until the presence feels most real.

Now, ask this person for forgiveness. Bring to mind something you did, or said, or didn't do, or didn't say, that caused pain to your loved one. Recall the incident as vividly as you can. Recall the sights, sounds, and smells associated with that time.

Tell him you are sorry about this, that you regret having caused him pain. Ask him to forgive you and to release you and to release himself from all the negativity associated with that time. Feel yourself being forgiven.

Next, recall a time when this person hurt you. Remember it as vividly as you can. Remember the sights, smells, and sounds. You may become emotional;

that's fine. Notice the emotions. Notice how they feel in your body. Keep breathing. If the emotions get too strong, do another series of seven breaths to the base of the spine. After you have recalled as much as you can of the painful time, look closely at your loved one. Tell him, "I forgive your for _____, and in forgiving you, I release you and I release myself." Notice how you feel in your body. Notice any feeling of lightness. Notice the pain leaving your heart.

Breathe.

Now, remember the loving times. Remember the close times. Make them vivid in your mind. Remember how things smelled. Remember the tastes. Remember the sights and sounds associated with your best times together. Now, smile with your own heart and say, "Thank you." See him smiling back at you. Float for a moment, and be in the presence of the love between you.

Breathe.

Now, smile deeply at your loved one. Feel your heart-space opening wider and wider. It may feel sore. It may feel scary. Just allow it to open more and more with each inhalation. When your heart is open, breathe in all that forgiveness, all those memories (the good and the bad), and all the love between you. Take at least seven breaths, gathering it all up in your heart.

Look again at your loved one. Feel the sadness of this parting. Let your heart slowly encircle the things you have taken in. Notice your loved one slowly, slowly floating away. And say, "Goodbye."

Completing the Developmental Tasks of Life

To everything there is a season

And a time for every purpose under heaven

—*Ecclesiastes*

A life well-lived includes the successful navigation of difficult times, the gathering of wisdom, and the ability to face fear, pain, and death itself without being overcome. Your loved one must finish the developmental tasks of life before he can address the final tasks of his life. What was started must be completed; closure must be obtained in some way, if only to talk about the unfinished tasks and dreams.

Look for guidance for these tasks in history and stories, as well as in your own experiences. Many of our traditional folktales speak in parables of the phases and tasks of this temporal life.

One simple way to help your loved one complete his tasks is to help him recognize the significant themes that ran through his life. For example, he may have had a constant struggle with money. Or perhaps as a child, he experienced the same conflicts with his parents that he felt with his own children when he became a parent. Many people find themselves faced with the same themes in different relationships. They may say something like, "I keep marrying the same man!" We all have themes that run through our lives that prompt us to say, "I thought I was finished with that years ago! Now here it is again!"

Themes are those aspects in life that make you feel unlucky, or as though you have had to grapple with the same issue again and again. But there are also positive themes in everyone's life: the areas in which you are lucky, blessed, or when things happen with ease. Don't forget to include the positive themes in life as you and your loved one realize the common threads that tied his life together.

Helping your loved one in this way helps him understand the role that these themes played in his growth and development. As he approaches death, the themes can serve as an overlay for his experiences, so he can sort it all out. Upon seeing the bigger picture, he'll be more complete with his developmental tasks and be more able to face the task of coming to the end of his life.

The Search for Authenticity

"What is *real?*" asked the Rabbit one day…

"Does it mean having things that buzz inside you

and a stick out handle?" "Real isn't how you are made," said

the Skin Horse, "It's a thing that happens to you."

—*Margery Williams,*
"The Velveteen Rabbit"

We have spoken about life review and the need, at the end of life, for the moments of our days to come together—to pattern themselves so that they give way to meaning and value. One of the most important tasks at the end of life is to determine the purpose of our sojourn, and to find completion. This sense of purpose and completion will serve to illuminate the final twists and turns of our life path. Death brings with it a hunger for absolute truth, for total authenticity.

This quest for authenticity—the need to know what is *real* about our lives—is a recurring theme. Sometimes it happens at the very end of our days, but if we are very fortunate, the process of sorting begins earlier, when there is still time to change course.

Patty

For Patty, it began with a biopsy. "The fear sort of crept up on me," she says now. It started innocently enough with her yearly Pap test. Then came the call from her physician's office. It was probably nothing to worry about, they told her, but they wanted her to have a biopsy early the following week. She went. Although she wasn't outwardly worried, the very act of undergoing these tests set into motion an internal process of preparing for death.

In the days that she waited for her test results, questions emerged: questions about the meaning of her endeavors, and about the quality and depth of her personal relationships.

Except for a brief marriage in her early twenties, Patty had been single all her adult life. She was a teacher and had been very career-driven. Patty had often sacrificed friendships and love relationships for her career. She now began to examine these decisions.

"I know I was a good teacher," she said later. "The kids benefited from me. It always felt more like a 'calling' than a career. It gave power to me and meaning to my life."

Patty had been dating Steve for three years. Like her, he was very focused on his career. In recent years, Steve's professional life had taken off, and he was finally getting the recognition and the financial rewards for which he had long worked. Between his career and other obligations, this left little time for his relationship with Patty.

Despite some occasional pangs of need and seasonal yearnings for more connection, Patty had never seriously questioned the relationship. She didn't think much about it at all—at least not until she felt the whisperings of Death over her left shoulder. And like the old Peggy Lee ballad, Patty began to wonder, "Is this all there is?"

It was during the holidays that Patty asked Steve the questions she had been afraid to ask before, and she listened quietly to the answers she had been afraid to hear. Did he love her? Probably. Was he in love with her? No, not in the way she wanted to be loved. He hadn't even loved his ex-wife like that, he said.

Why had these questions emerged now? What precipitated the need to know answers to painful questions, which had for so long been avoided?

"I just had to know," Patty explains. "I was sitting there not knowing whether I was going to be around next year. And suddenly I wanted to know the truth about my life. Understanding what our relationship had been for Steve was a piece of information I needed to know. I also needed to know what this had been about for me."

Patty spent most of that week digging deeply into her life, examining her choices, and weaving her experiences into a well-told story with a beginning, a middle, and the start of a resolution. "It's in the last chapter," she says, "that everything comes together and begins to make sense."

As things turned out, Patty's biopsy was negative. She went forward into her life with a sense of relief and resolve that had not been there previously. Her journey into the final chapter was enormously valuable. It brought a focus and clarity to the underpinnings of her professional and personal decisions.

These days, Patty puts more energy into her social life, and she values the decisions she made with regard to her career. "I love my work," she told us, "and I feel that teaching is more than just my profession. It's my contribution to the world. It is an expression of my soul."

She continues to process her relationship with Steve. It's hard. "I used to have fantasies about him," she says. "I used to think things would be different somehow if I was his wife. Now I know that I don't want that. I want a man who really loves me, and Steve can't do that."

Patty's fleeting encounter with her mortality set into motion an intense and brutal self-examination. Although she will continue to struggle with the issues that revolve around Steve, her priorities, her values, and her needs are clearly defined. They have become part of her life map. She is already moving on.

Briefly the veil parted,

illusion faded

revealing the Unity

and Mystery

some call God

—*Patrick W. Flanigan, MD*

"Surviving the Storm"

Acceptance and Acknowledgment

Hope is the thing with feathers

That perches in the soul…

That sings

The tune without the words

And never stops, at all

—Emily Dickinson

In our culture, "acceptance" implies understanding, agreement, or at least compliance. Acceptance is a laudable goal. Acceptance comes after much painful soul-searching. For better or worse, we have found peace with the enormity of our loss and the fragments of our lives (and of dying) are beginning to come together. However, the mother who has lost her child may never understand, may never agree, or may never comply. What has occurred will never be okay with her. You may never accept the loss of your loved one. Edgar Allen Poe's poem, "Annabel Lee," speaks of a longing that will never cease.

Annabel Lee

It was many and many a year ago

In a kingdom by the sea

That a maiden there lived that you may know

By the name of Annabel Lee.

And this maiden she lived with no other thought

Than to love and be loved by me.

I was a child and she was a child,

In this kingdom by the sea

But we loved with a love that was more than a love—

I and my Annabel Lee—

With a love that the winged Seraphs in Heaven

Coveted her and me.

And that is the reason that long ago,

In this kingdom by the sea

A wind blew out of a cloud, chilling

My beautiful Annabel Lee...

...But our love it was stronger by far than the love

Of those who are older than we

Of many far wiser than we—

Neither the Angels in Heaven above

Nor the demons down under the sea,

Can ever dissever my soul from the soul

Of the beautiful Annabel Lee—

For the moon never beams without bringing me dreams

Of the beautiful Annabel Lee—

And the stars never rise but I feel the bright eyes

Of the beautiful Annabel Lee—

And so, all the night-tide, l lie down by the side

Of my darling—my darling—my life

and my bride,

In her sepulcher there by the sea—

In her tomb by the sounding sea.

—*Edgar Allen Poe*

Perhaps *acknowledgment* may be more helpful in this context. Acknowledgment only validates the reality of what has happened or what is happening. Acknowledgment is the vehicle by which the gravity of the loss and the severity of the pain can be woven into the greater context of our lives without the need to agree. We know that life will never be the same. And we know that life will continue.

Love has gone and left me, and the neighbors

Knock and

Borrow,

And life goes on forever like the gnawing of a

Mouse.

And to-morrow and to-morrow and to-morrow

There's this little street and this little house.

—*Edna St. Vincent Millay*

Acknowledgment does not imply consent. Sometimes acknowledgment is all that we can ask for or achieve. And given the tasks of grief, acknowledgment is a more realistic and achievable goal. In acknowledging our losses and grief, we are empowered to continue with our lives, however diminished we may feel. Acknowledgment can help usher in the agreement needed for the growth toward acceptance. The gift of acknowledgment is tomorrow.

Father Jan

Father Jan Stasiak was a retired Catholic priest. He had been a parish priest in Oakland and the East Bay for over thirty years. He emigrated from his native Poland in the early fifties and became a beloved priest in his community. He retired to the Monterey Peninsula and lived there with his caregiver of many years. I felt privileged when he and his caregiver came to my office for health care.

Father Jan was a physical train wreck. He had smoked unfiltered cigarettes for many years, drank for as many years, all the while eating a basic European diet: fat, lard, calories, and cheese. Father Jan thought that going on a diet meant cutting back to three strips of bacon, four eggs, and three sausages every morning—washed down with Italian coffee and heavy cream. The concept of physical exercise was foreign to Father Jan.

He came to me with no particular complaints, except for the shortness of breath upon climbing the stairs for this office visit. I tried, but could not impress upon Father Jan that he had the potential to become very ill and that he should modify what he considered a well-deserved lifestyle. And so I played catch up with Father Jan, trying to stay on top of his current medical problems.

As time went on and his habits remained the same, the shortness of breath progressed, requiring more and stronger inhalers. He began with Theodur (a medicine to help him breathe better), and eventually I put him on steroids. Chronic obstructive pulmonary disease (COPD), commonly known as emphysema, is an insidiously progressive disease, and it takes no rest. (In the army we would say "Take no prisoners" or "Take names and kick butt.")

And because of its relentless nature, my overriding concern was that Father Jan was soon going to have congestive heart failure—probably on a Monday morning following one of his weekend salt-and-sausage fests. He was also on a diuretic and electrolyte replacement. Father Jan developed an irregular heartbeat, requiring digoxin (a medicine to slow his fast and erratic heartbeat and to strengthen the heart contractions) and a medicine for the accompanying high blood pressure. These measures managed to keep Father Jan tuned up, and he did okay for a while. But it wasn't long before he began showing up in the emergency room at night with difficulty breathing.

He was seventy-four and on a cholesterol-lowering therapy when he had his first heart attack. Although seventy-four isn't old by today's standards, the temptations of homemade sausage, fresh butter, and heavy cream were quickly aging him, and slowly winning the battle for his health.

One day he came to my office and said, "Doc, I am having a hard time singing in the church choir. I have sung like a lark for years, but now my voice is changing." And it was true: he did sound different. A trip to the ear, nose, and throat specialist showed a lesion on one of Father Jan's vocal cords and paralysis of the other one. A biopsy revealed cancer of the vocal cords with metastasis to the voice box. He underwent surgery and radiation therapy and was back to singing within six months. He had an iron constitution, this man of God from Poland.

Then one Christmas he visited me again, this time complaining that he had difficulty passing urine. Six months earlier his prostate gland had been normal, and tests had shown everything was normal.

Now, on re-examination, his prostate gland was huge and rock-hard and his PSA level (a chemical that gets higher with prostate cancer) was very high. After a quick referral to the urologist, Father Jan chose radiation therapy as his only course of treatment, stating, "No surgery for me. Once was enough."

After a discussion with the oncologist, he did agree to some chemotherapy. His other diseases were stable, meaning they were at an acceptable level for him, but certainly not for me. However, the treatment was his choice. This was his body and his life to live.

By 1996, he had become totally enthralled with the idea of returning to his native Poland at the same time the pope would be there. That was, after all, where the pope had blessed him in the 1940s and where he wanted to be blessed again. He asked if he could survive the trip and how he could get his medications into Poland.

"What are your plans?" I asked. "Are you coming back?" He didn't answer. "How long do you want to stay there?" He wasn't sure. He was only concerned with getting home, seeing the pope, and being at his birthplace. It occurred to me that he had decided to go home to die. I didn't ask him about that, but now I feel that I should have. I told Father Jan that I would ship the necessary medications every three months, or give him a year's supply to take with him. He chose the latter option.

Before leaving, Father Jan told me that without my help and understanding, life would not have been complete. He considered me a "divine part of the plan for his life." It was mutual. I had always thought of him as a father figure, albeit a stubborn one. Indeed, I had received great strength from our relationship, and felt fortunate to have been able to care for Father Jan.

It was a labor of love for me, and somehow, when Father Jan left that day, we both knew it was the last time we would see each other. With tears in our eyes, the father thanked me profusely for all I had done, and we hugged good-bye. The moment was truly one of connection—a time when words could not express what we felt in our hearts. We knew we were losing each other. Father Jan was being lost to the rituals of life and to the need to do what he must. I was losing a beloved patient, and a piece of my heart.

I have always found it difficult to hide behind a mantle of professional objectivity and indifference. I just wade right in there, emote, and cry with my patients. I am not only a physician. "Doctor" is a professional designation—one of which I am proud. But first and foremost, I am a person. After all, I have been a human being much longer than I have been a doctor. I have to be honest with myself and my patients about my feelings. The fact that Father Jan was preparing to die also occurred to me, but I had a difficult time accepting his matter-of-fact approach to planning it. He had accepted his death so fully that it almost seemed that he wanted to die. I admit that I was angry with him about that. "Why didn't you let me help you fight some more?" I asked him once in frustration. "Life is a precious gift."

Father Jan only smiled and replied quietly, "Sometimes, so is death."

"You're right, Father," I answered. "We don't want to prolong death. Suffering must end. You have made the right choice."

Once I had worked through this, I felt much better, and even strangely happy for Father Jan. I felt blessed to have had a part in his life. I learned more about myself, by watching the way he lived in the face of death, than about anyone else. Father Jan did all this as a matter of course, planning in detail and dealing with it with his usual zest and love for life.

And so Father Jan left my life.

I thought of him often as time went on, and wondered what had happened to him. Not long after he left, I was privileged to be in Germany with the US Army for five months. While there, I couldn't get him out of my mind. I thought about going to the town in Poland to find him. I was much too busy with my work, however, and had no time to locate him. I returned home disappointed that I had not been able to do it.

As I was restarting my private practice, I learned that none of my associates had seen or heard from Father Jan. His caregiver had also disappeared. Time passed, and he became a pleasant memory. Whenever I felt depressed, I thought of this wonderful, zesty, crusty retired priest who bore the heavy burden of life-threatening illnesses. He faced them head-on, never flinching, never complaining. He just lived life as it was handed to him. He had probably known that he was going to die soon and decided that it was going to happen in his native Poland, near his birthplace and after he saw the pope.

Some months after I came back from Europe, my wife and I drove to Oakland in the East Bay to visit dear friends who had moved there. We arrived early and sat in front of their apartment building, chatting and reading every newspaper and magazine we could find by the mailboxes. One of the papers was the *Mont-clairion*, a weekly neighborhood newspaper filled with local gossip and news. Several pages inside, I found a picture that looked familiar. The headline above the picture said: *Beloved Father Jan Stasiak, retired priest from our local parish, dies in Poland.* It went on to say that Father Jan had retired to the Monterey Bay area, that he had become ill, and that he had returned to his native Poland to see his birthplace and the visiting holy father, who had blessed him.

At long last I knew what had happened to Father Jan. I almost became unraveled. I believe in what I term "loop completion" and synchronicity, but this seemed a miracle. The rest of the evening was a blur. I was ecstatic, being with my dear friends and finally knowing what had happened to Father Jan. He had done it! I only hope I can do it that well when my time comes.

Final Loss of Authority and Change in Family Role

As a person moves from diagnosis toward death, there is an inexorable loss of strength, physical appearance, and function. Competence and capability flounder. Strength wanes. The body fails. People who once led independent lives now find themselves relying on others for basic life functions.

When family and loved ones become the caregivers for a dying person, there is a gradual change in family role and a shift in authority. The mother of three young adults may stare in disbelief as her thirty-five-year-old daughter cajoles her to eat all her dinner. A successful attorney who sent his son to an Ivy League graduate school may hear that same son telling him, "I'm going to handle the money for you, Dad. You forgot to pay the mortgage last month. Don't worry. I'll take care of everything."

This reversal of roles is a difficult one and must be executed with the utmost love and sensitivity. This is another time when you can draw on Rilke's *unknowing* so that this delicate role change can be integrated with care.

Many of your newer roles will be negotiated with your loved one *before* he becomes unable to do those things for himself. This helps to ease the trauma of what he may view as iniquities.

Your dying loved one is losing a part of his perceived self. He is relinquishing his sense of competence in the world. It is a searing experience, often involving great struggle and personal tumult. Longstanding relationships are severely challenged. Yet this time of pain and loss holds the potential for enormous healing. Most people *want* to heal the past, and these vulnerable times provide an opportunity to do it.

Love will get you through this, too.

References and Readings

Susan Seldon Boulet and Michael Babcock, <u>The Goddess Painting</u>, Pomegranate Art Books, Rhonert Park, 1994.

Jean Shinoda Bolen, MD, <u>Goddesses in Every Woman</u>, Harper and Row, New York, 1984.

Byock, Ira, "When Suffering Persists," *Journal of Palliative Care,* 1994, Vol. 10, No 2, pp. 8-13.

Byock, Ira, <u>Dying Well,</u> Putnam Books, New York, 1997.

Cassell, Eric, "A Simplified Description of the Person," in <u>The Nature of Suffering and the Goals of Medicine</u>, The Oxford Press, Oxford, England.

R.M. Rilke, <u>Selected Poems to Rainer Maria Rilke.</u> translation by Bly, Harper and Row, 1996.

Myss, Caroline, <u>Anatomy of the Spirit</u>, Three Rivers Press, New York. 1996.

6

JANUARY AND FEBRUARY

But February made me shiver

With every paper I'd deliver

Bad news on the doorstep

Couldn't take one more step

—Don McLean

This is the time of the turn toward dying. It is an active time for growth at the end of life. Death has been acknowledged and accepted. Many preparations have been made. Much has been accomplished. There comes a moment when your loved one turns away from actively living and begins actively dying. This season comprises a major transition between the epiphanies and miracles experienced during the festival of winter lights and a gradual turning away from the waning life. This includes the waning of the physical body, the waning social life, and the loss of all other relationships. The soul itself is beginning to *pull anchor* and is getting ready to divest itself from the energy of this life. The process is not a steady march toward death, but it is a relentless one. The will to live or die fluctuates through the passing seasons of dying. It may depend on the preparation that you, your loved one, the rest of the family, and the caregivers have made together as a team. By the time your loved one is ready to die, peace is accompanied by readiness, and a calm expectation of moving on is present.

Depression and Detachment

I see a red door

I must have it painted black

No colors anymore

I want them to turn black.

—*The Rolling Stones*

Depression is the final surrender to hopelessness. It is the black pit from which acceptance comes. In the sinking down and the climbing out, your loved one achieves the goal of separation. Depression is quintessential solitude. Depression is painful for your loved one and for you. This may be his first realization that, despite the family and friends gathered at the bedside, his journey will be a solitary one. For you, it can be a foretaste of future feelings of despair and detachment.

This is the hour of lead

Remembered if outlived

As freezing persons recollect the snow

First chill, then stupor, then the letting go

—*Emily Dickinson*

Depression is profoundly solitary. It is, as Dickinson so eloquently states, "the hour of lead." One of the most painful qualities of depression is the nearly total feeling of disconnection you and your loved one may feel from each other and from the outside world. Even one's normal sense of time and season is altered. *This has neither wax nor wane, neither stop nor start.* It can be difficult to remember other times, other emotions. It is often impossible to believe that lives will mend and routines will begin to feel normal again, that the world can ever again be whole. A more helpful label for this period may be detachment.

Sorrow

Sorrow like a ceaseless rain

Beats upon my heart.

People twist and scream in pain—

Dawn will find them still again;

This has neither wax nor wane

Neither stop nor start.

—*Edna St Vincent Millay*

In her book, "Why People Don't Heal, and How They Can" (Harmony Books, 1997), Dr. Carolyn Myss speaks of a need to return to the wound to recover lost energy and to heal. This return to the wound, or source of the suffering, is a recurrent theme in our literature. Our religious texts contain many stories of depression, detachment, surrender, and resurrection. These are metaphors for dying.

The Torah speaks of the Children of Israel's forty-year sojourn into the desert. The spiritual development of Judaism and the foundation of Judeo-Christian thought emerged from the wanderings. This was the time of the Torah. It was in the desert that the laws emerged. This is where the holy covenant was entered, where the ark was constructed, and where the despair that spawned the culture of the golden calf gradually transformed itself into self-reliance, courage, and hopefulness. God promised the Israelites that he would make them a holy people. He accomplished this by taking them on a long and arduous pilgrimage through desolate terrain. The Torah teaches us that it is through the journey itself that the Promised Land is manifested. "He found him in a desert region, in an empty, howling waste." (Deuteronomy 32:9–10)

The Christian account of the incident at the garden of Gethsemane speaks of a period of despair, which Dickinson calls "the hour of lead." This time of sadness, confusion, and fear is not presented as a symptom to be treated or a phase to be overcome. The hour of lead is a precondition of the transformation itself.

Allegories about transformation are not unique to Western religious traditions. A Native American healer Pam met once gave the gift of his wisdom in these matters in a small rock shop in Berkeley on a rainy Sunday afternoon:

Pam was sitting on the floor, sorting through the tumbled stones in a large barrel when an old Indian came in and sat beside her. He sat quietly for a while, observing her, making her a little uncomfortable. Finally, he spoke.

"You are troubled," he said. He was right.

"I will give you the solution," he said. "The solution to your problem is in the problem itself. Do not look elsewhere for the solution. The answer is always in the question. The healing is always in the wound. The way out is always in."

Your loved one is disengaging from you, leaving you to embark on a solitary journey into his darker places. Such an act of abandonment generates in you a fear of your own aloneness. Because of your own fears, you may not see the vision quest or the sacredness of your loved one's journey. Sometimes, either because of fear or out of our love and natural desire to protect our loved ones, we circumvent this process. The symptoms of detachment may be wrongly perceived as an illness. Sometimes we impede the path with chemical antidepressants and misdirected talking therapies designed to cure a process that is not a disease. Detachment is not depression. And depression is not sadness. Sadness is a normal response to a difficult or painful situation. Depression occurs when symptoms that are consistent with sadness persist and become so overbearing that there is a sense of despair and hopelessness. Although detachment can sometimes be a symptom of depression, it is not the condition itself. Don't inadvertently call your loved one back from this journey. He needs to reach his center. He needs to complete the mission that propelled this sacred adventure. In withholding passage, we deny our loved ones the gift of arrival.

A woman spoke to us once of sitting with her husband whose detachment was reaching completion: emotionally, physically, and spiritually. He was in a deep and impenetrable coma. As she sat at his bedside, she became aware of the pattern of his breathing. It was shallow and quick. She began, slowly at first, to follow the pattern of his breathing with her own breathing. It took several minutes to synchronize her breath with his. But finally they were as one breath in the room.

"I felt so close to him," she told us. "I had finally found a way to be with him again."

We have done this ourselves as a way of connecting with someone who was quickly leaving. It helped us feel and acknowledge the depth of caring that exists between us all. Remember this, as it may also mitigate your own sense of isolation and fear.

End-of-life depression is necessary, and it may last a long or short while. But if you know it is a part of the dying process, then you will be prepared to deal with it. Ultimately, it results in more freedom for your loved one.

Detachment at the end of life does not interfere with a person's life tasks. It defines them. Life isn't random and meaningless—no matter how it may feel while in the throes of the pain and fear. *The way out is always in. And the gift of detachment is arrival.*

Managing Feelings of Helplessness

Most of us go about our daily lives as though we could predict, even control, the outcome. We change the lighting and temperature of a room with the flick of a switch. We care for our children and provide for our families with almost-perfect confidence in our ability to ensure a secure environment, a good experience, a safe world. Most of the time, for most of us, this is our truth about life. We are in control. Nothing unexpected will happen.

Then something unexpected and unacceptable happens. A child vanishes into the night. A hurricane throws city buildings around as though they were children's blocks, leaving the world strewn across the landscape like a nursery playroom. For you, the world began to career out of control when you heard the news that your loved one has a terminal illness.

You cannot control your loved one's illness. You cannot control the rate of physical decline he experiences. You cannot control his experience of the illness, nor his reaction to it. You *can,* however, influence his experience of his illness. You can also control your own responses to the pain and chaos that surrounds you.

With this in mind, and while acknowledging the feelings of helplessness you will often experience, we offer the following suggestions to restore some sense of balance and competence in a dizzying world.

- **Be aware of your own physical sensations and reactions to anxiety and fear.** Some people experience palpitations, hyperventilation, sweating, chills, ringing in their ears, digestive problems, or other physical symptoms. While these are natural responses to stress, they can add to your feelings of chaos.

- **Find ways to manage those physical reactions.** Sometimes sudden panic or overwhelming emotion can cause palpitations, or rapid heartbeat. This in turn can cause you to breathe too fast or too hard, which leads to hyperventilation. You may also experience ringing in your ears. For any of these conditions, sit down and deliberately slow down your breathing. Breathe slowly and steadily until the symptoms subside. If you feel dizzy, lie down or lower your head toward your lap. As the blood returns to your head, you should feel more stable. If you continue to hyperventilate, put a paper bag over your mouth and nose and breathe in and out of it. This sounds silly, but it works. And remember, if your hyperventilation continues and you pass out, you will simply revert back to normal breathing. It only *feels* scary. Many people perspire when they are frightened. It's usually a chilly or clammy kind of sweat. Usually temperature fluctuations only affect arms and legs. This is the body's way of defending itself in a primitive readiness for fight or flight. All the available blood contracts into the trunk of the body to protect the vital organs. This is also why you may notice goose bumps on your arms and legs, even if you are sweating. The perspiration is often accompanied by shaking and feeling weak in the arms or legs. In this case, the best thing to do is to relax and warm up in a tepid (not hot) bath. Adding a handful of lavender bath salts will go a long way toward soothing your jangled nerves. Since bathing isn't always possible, carry along an extra sweater or shawl for these occasions. Carrying an extra garment is easier and more comfortable than overdressing—especially since you may be in hospitals or medical offices that are very warm. Digestive problems are another common symptom of stress. Some people experience sharp abdominal pain, diarrhea or constipation. Clearly, this is why it's important to maintain a healthy diet. Sometimes the temptation to skip eating or to eat sweets and fast foods takes over, but eating poorly can wreak havoc on your digestion. During these times of stress, stick with your usual eating patterns if they are good, or develop healthier patterns for the time being. Alcohol can irritate the stomach lining, leading to nausea and vomiting. If you have ulcers, alcohol will make them worse. Certain pain medications and sedatives can cause constipation. This is the time to listen to your body and treat yourself well. If these symptoms persist, see your physician. And remember, all of the symptoms we have discussed can also be signs of serious medical conditions. If you have a medical history symptomatic of any of the conditions described above, you need to check with your doctor.

- **Remember your strengths.** Even when you can't change a situation, you *can* influence it. You can offer your understanding, your compassion and your love. You can offer forgiveness. Sometimes humor can lighten the load. Or you can simply offer your prayers.

- **Be of assistance.** Getting outside of yourself and your own thoughts can be the best way to help yourself. Offer someone else a massage, a hug, or a word of encouragement. (You can also ask for these things for yourself.) If your loved one is in pain, bring him his medications, call his physician, or consult with his hospice nurse. You are not helpless. Do the things you *can* do.

- **Stay in the present.** There *are* ways to heal the pain and anger rooted in the past. You *can* find ways to make the future less searing and more meaningful. But the tools to do those things are in the *present*. The focus of all your power is in the present, and that is where you must begin.

Getting Help

At this point, your loved one can be totally dependent. You may need to recruit help. Caring for the dying is grueling, both physically and mentally. No one person can provide this level of care around the clock. Your loved one's needs can be overwhelming. Furthermore, it may be best to engage help, in order to protect her dignity and to preserve the personal nature of your relationship.

A dying parent, for example, receiving intensely personal physical care from a child often feels humiliated. Recruiting someone outside the family for this kind of care can honor the dignity of the parent. Discuss this with your loved one and the other caretakers, then decide what is best for all concerned.

If a family is totally consumed with providing physical care, resentments can build. This can get in the way of what's important in this end-of-life journey.

We spoke earlier of getting help from hospice agencies. By the time your loved one is this dependent, and if you have not already gotten home-care assistance, now is the time. If you have home care in place, you may want to speak with your case manager and physician about finding a hospice and switching the mode of care to their expertise. This will enable you to dwell in the emotional and spiritual issues, rather than attending to the often-unpleasant physical needs.

If your loved one's finances are not in order, this may be the last opportunity to finalize those arrangements. If he's not in the state of mind to make good decisions, and the financial picture is simple and straightforward, consider assigning a family member to take over general power of attorney. You can pick up the general power of attorney form in any full-service stationery store. If finances are complex, your attorney or financial planner will be able to assist. In either situation, your loved one will have to sign the papers, and it will need to be notarized.

These issues, though difficult and sometimes embarrassing, are very important and will directly affect what funds are available at the time of death. After an individual dies, banks and financial institutions may freeze the accounts, pending probate. If accounts are held jointly, or if there is a power of attorney, funds can be released.

If the prospect of organizing your loved one's financial matters is too daunting, do what you need to do: get help.

Medical Equipment

You will need more than additional people to assist you. You will also need durable medical equipment in your home to make caregiving easier.

A hospital bed with side rails and an air mattress are common household items in this stage of a dying person's life. People often become agitated at the end of life, and sometimes they attempt to get out of bed when they are clearly not strong enough to walk. They may also toss and turn more while asleep, and the risk of falling out of bed increases. Hospital beds can be adjusted for the comfort of the patient, enabling a better chance at good rest and sound sleep. The beds are also made to elevate and drop, making it easier to reach and bend during bed baths and other care. An air mattress or foam egg-crate mattress will alleviate the potential for bedsores. Even so, you may still need to help your loved one change position.

"Draw sheets" are one way that you can reposition him more easily. A draw sheet is simply a flat sheet folded in half or in thirds, lengthwise. It is placed across the middle of the bed with the ends tucked under the sides of the mattress. With one person on each side of the patient, the draw sheet can be untucked and used to lift and move the patient, even if he is very weak. If your loved one is incontinent, the draw sheet will save you having to change entire sets of bed linens. You can also purchase disposable pads for incontinence.

A medical trapeze over the top of the bed is another helpful device. The individual can grasp the trapeze bar or triangle and therefore assist while bed linens are changed, while using the bedpan, or simply in order to change positions.

A Place to Die

We acknowledged earlier that it might not be possible for your loved one to die at home. There may not be sufficient caregivers available, or the only caregiver might be elderly or infirm himself. Or there simply might not be anyone around who can give the kind of care that's required in the situation. This is the time to be sure that you have thoroughly explored all your community resources and that you understand how to access and utilize these services, in order to get the maximum assistance through this period.

Sometimes the myriad of choices can be confusing, especially when emotions are high and sleep is scarce. What follows is a brief description of basic services and facilities that may be available in your community. We discussed them earlier. Now is the time to review what may be available.

- **Residential care homes.** Many elderly people, particularly those suffering from Alzheimer's disease, already live in residential care settings. These small facilities have become "home" to your loved one. Usually there is no need for him to be moved to another level of care as death approaches. Hospice care can be delivered to the residential care home.

- **Skilled nursing facilities.** Also known as convalescent hospitals or nursing homes, these facilities provide nursing care and have a registered nurse on staff twenty-four hours a day. They also provide physical and occupational therapy, and social work services. Many skilled nursing hospitals have contractual agreements with local hospice providers for end-of-life care for their residents. The cost of hospice services when provided in a nursing home are covered by Medicare and Medicare HMOs. The cost of the residential services themselves (room and board rate) is borne by the patient.

- **Hospitals.** If the community does not have adequate facilities to care for dying people, the hospital becomes the only option. Some hospitals have palliative care teams, who deliver comprehensive symptom management and end-of-life care.

- **Hospice houses.** Some communities are fortunate enough to have inpatient hospice facilities. Their services may vary according to financial resources. In San Francisco, for instance, a patient can go to a residential hospice facility as soon as he qualifies for hospice care (that is, when a doctor certifies that he is not expected to live more than six months). Some hospice care facilities admit patients who are ambulatory, can have guests, and who participate in the community. In other facilities, the individual must be actively dying to be eligible for care. Check with your doctor or the local hospice agency. They are listed in the yellow pages, and any social worker will be able to connect you with a hospice.

- **Respite care.** Some families agree that the loved one will remain at home and have a home death. But the caregivers need a break. Hospice agencies offer respite care in local skilled nursing facilities and, on occasion, in hospitals. Your loved one would then be cared for at a local hospital or nursing home for a brief time while you catch your breath.

Loss of Bodily Functions

As death gets closer, the ability to control body functions declines. Your loved one may be incontinent and have to wear diapers. She may be unable to chew or swallow; she may be unable to digest what you offer so lovingly. Strong emotional support and spiritual resources will be needed to allow you and your loved one to cope with this dramatic stage of decline.

Throughout all of the other losses you as a caregiver suffered, your challenge has been to rethink who you are, and to redefine the criteria from which you draw self-esteem. The work is not over yet. The criteria will change again now that the person you love and care for is losing control of her body. This is the time when there is no physical evidence left to help define who your loved one is. You can no longer describe her as having beautiful sparkling eyes, a radiant smile, or thick and sensuous hair. She can no longer define herself this way either. As her life dissolves, her physical presence is merely a shadow without capacity or substance. She is very close to becoming a purely spiritual entity.

From Self-Care to Dependence

From the discussions above, you see that the day will likely come when your loved one will be in a wheelchair or be bed bound, will have to be in a wheelchair, or might be bedridden. You might move a hospital bed into the house and place a commode nearby, or perhaps a bedpan is all you'll need. These steps indicate that your loved one depends on you, other family members, friends, and caretakers. You'll work together to prepare meals, do the dressing and bathing, and perhaps even toileting. As your loved one becomes increasingly more dependent upon those who care for him, you may witness changes in his thought process, alertness, and moods.

Being dependent, needing assistance from others for dressing, bathing, and attending to the most personal and intimate aspects of personal hygiene can be humiliating and overwhelming. How can this be a time of healing?

Marcy

Marcy was a nurse in a Midwestern hospital. She worked the swing shift in the emergency room, raised three energetic daughters during the day, and slept whenever she could. Marcy's husband, Sid, was a carpenter. He was a kind and hardworking man. Over the years, their dual career and split-shift lifestyle had taken a toll on their marriage. By the time the children were raised and gone, Marcy and Sid were more like housemates than life-mates. They shared the house and nodded pleasantries to each other as they crossed paths, but lived totally separate lives.

Seven years ago, Marcy was diagnosed with breast cancer. She underwent a modified radical mastectomy of her right breast. After surgery, Marcy undertook a grueling course of chemotherapy followed by radiation. It was a difficult and arduous treatment.

Marcy's strength had always been in her competence. Even in her debilitated physical condition, Marcy managed and supervised her way through. She organized friends into car pools that transported her to therapy appointments. She kept a detailed notebook with questions for her physicians, and painstakingly recorded her changing condition. She researched all the current literature on breast cancer. She took charge of every aspect of her treatment and recovery. We used to joke that she didn't so much recover, but instead smacked the cancer into submission.

On the fifth anniversary of Marcy's remission, we celebrated at a luncheon in suburban Chicago. Pam remarked on her courage during the ordeal.

"You were so amazingly courageous," Pam said. "A real example for the rest of us."

Marcy looked incredulous. "Brave? I wish I'd been really brave. I wish I'd been brave enough to let somebody—anybody—know how scared I was."

This revelation took Pam by surprise.

"Surely you told someone," Pam said. "I mean, Sid knew, didn't he?"

Marcy shook her head. "Sid probably knew less than you did. I used to get scared at night. I used to cry when I went to bed. But his room is on the other side of the house. He never heard me." She took a sip of wine and leaned over the table toward Pam, whispering, "You know, he's never even seen the mastectomy scar."

Late that summer Marcy had a recurrence of her cancer, with lesions in the left breast. Tests showed widely metastatic disease with lesions in the bone, in the lung, and in her brain. The doctors told her that the cancer was spreading very quickly. She was given a prognosis of less than six months to live.

Marcy's symptoms grew worse following her diagnosis. She developed excruciating pain in her back that could only be relieved with strong narcotics. Her strength waned. Sometimes it was too difficult to get out of bed, even for meals. Finally, hospice care was ordered.

One autumn day, Marcy was lying on the couch, staring out the window at the falling foliage. "Do you remember my remission party," she asked Pam, "when I told you how scared I had been during treatment? You didn't tell anyone else, did you?"

As Marcy continued to decline, we ordered a hospital bed and placed it in the living room where the couch had been, so she could continue to enjoy the view of the autumn colors. We put a walker next to the bed. With help from Sid, she was able, for a time, to get to the bathroom. As her strength declined, she became unable to walk the short distance to the bathroom, even with Sid's help. He ordered a bedside commode. Sid had to empty it, and as her disease progressed, he had to help her on and off the commode. Finally, Marcy became completely incontinent.

Each of these changes and losses was met with struggle, resistance, and an overwhelming sense of personal degradation. And in each instance, Marcy lost the battle. With each defeat, she had to relinquish that piece of her autonomy, of her perceived dignity, of her attachment to authority in her life. It was a time of great pain and personal chaos.

Yet, concurrent with all these losses, in the midst of this struggle, subtle changes occurred between Marcy and Sid. It began with the walker. Sid would help Marcy out of bed, watch as she made her way through the living room, and sit patiently outside the bathroom door. Once in a while, he would tap on the door and ask, "Everything okay in there?" When the commode became a part of their lives, Sid would make small talk as he emptied and returned the container to her bedside. It seemed to ease her discomfort, and his own.

Once in a while, he would sit at her bedside and they would talk, sometimes for a few minutes, and other times long into the night.

When Marcy became incontinent and bed-bound, her care needs changed again. A home health aide came to assist with personal care. One afternoon, a few days before Marcy's death, the aide arrived at the house to find Marcy in a particularly upbeat mood. She was smiling and joking, more relaxed than she had been since the diagnosis. The aide made her a light lunch, which Marcy ate with enjoyment. Then the aide offered to change her sheets and give Marcy her bath.

"You can change the linens," Marcy told her. "But I don't need a bath. Sid bathed me this morning." She blushed a little and concluded, "It was really nice."

Marcy died the following Sunday afternoon. Sid and her daughters were at her bedside, holding her hand as she left.

Professional caregivers share a deep understanding that it is an honor and a blessing to care for the dying. It allows us to experience ourselves as competent, compassionate, and giving.

On the other hand, the patient is often fraught with feelings of fear and loss. Relinquishing authority and autonomy causes the death of an individual's perceived sense of self. Yet in this letting go, the dying begin to see clearly what and who they have always been.

A close friend of ours, who is a Hindu, gives this advice: "When Shiva, god of destruction, is knocking at the door, it is a wise person who opens the door and welcomes him into her life." She elaborates, "You must understand that if Shiva is at your door, he will come in, invited or not. How much easier it is to make him welcome; how much wiser to elicit his friendship."

In losing her struggles, Marcy finally allowed Sid to care for her. His care and concern made her feel safer, and it reminded her of another time in her life: a time when she had fallen in love with Sid. She remembered how happy she had been in those days—how special she had felt as a young bride, and how safe. In caring for Marcy, Sid was also reminded of how much he had loved her in the early years of their marriage. He had seen her differently then. He had seen her as beautiful and soft and delicate. And he remembered how much he had loved to touch her. Their late-night talks brought them close again, and reminded them of who they really were to themselves and to each other.

Assisted Suicide and Its Alternatives

This is a difficult subject. The mere idea of assisted suicide upsets some people. Others feel that it is a viable option, and make preparations to accomplish it quite matter-of-factly.

We believe that if a qualified hospice team or compassionate and knowledge-able physician is treating the dying individual, there will be no need for suicide. If your loved one is comfortable, and acknowledges and accepts death, *there is no need for suicide or to hasten death.* Pain and fear of pain are believed to be the most prevalent reasons people opt for suicide.

If you believe this is the case with your loved one, we urge you discuss this with your physician. If your doctor is not skilled or comfortable administering pain medication in clinically effective dosages, you can have the hospice medical director assume your loved one's care.

Prolonging Life and Letting Go

When your loved one is near death, you may be asked if you would like her to receive IV fluids or feedings. Neither of these measures will prevent death, though sometimes the moment of death can be temporarily delayed. This is a tough dilemma, because you want to help your loved one—but you certainly don't want the trauma of his pain to linger.

Our suggestion is to withhold intravenous hydration and nutrition. It does not contribute to your loved one's comfort and may well increase his discomfort. When a person's bowels and bladder are shutting down, the fluid can cause uncomfortable bloating, and make breathing more difficult. Without IV fluid or nourishment, your loved one will die in a relatively short time—usually between one and 14 days. During this time, he will drift in and out of consciousness, and typically has no interest in nourishment. If his mouth is dry, you can gently moisten his lips and around his gums with a special swab that is available almost everywhere. You can even use a cotton ball or a cotton swab.

If he is conscious and able to swallow, you can provide small sips of water or easily digested snacks. Gelatin, puddings, and Popsicles are often requested.

7

March 19

I see the world gradually turning into a wilderness. I hear the ever-approaching thunder which shall destroy us too…and yet, if I look into the heavens, I think that it will all come right, that this cruelty too will end, and that peace and tranquility will return.

—*Anne Frank, "The Diary of Anne Frank"*

The last day of winter: the soul is ready to transition and the body is ready to die. It is the time of the bridge-crossing. The caregivers will be the survivors and look toward their spring and summer. Life needs to be lived, and growth must continue.

> *The healing and transitioning of the soul and spirit, the resolution of impending death by the dying patient through life review towards creating a self-concept is also a bridge to synchronicity. The illness resulting in eventual death is, in reality, a vehicle that enhances healing in both the patient and the caregiver. The patient becomes the teacher to you, to the physician, and other caregivers so that they together can experience synchronicity and the transition of the soul and spirit.*
>
> —*Dieter Joeckel, MD, hospice physician*

A Time To Die: More Ready Than You Think

The actual death of your loved one can be a deeply healing and calming transitional experience. All the other seasons you've lived through have been preparing you for this final one. You have endured the emotional and physical fatigue to the point of exhaustion, and possibly beyond. You and your dying loved one have accomplished much in preparation for this final event. You have overcome many obstacles and challenges, and you probably are more ready now than you even know. Your acceptance and acknowledgment is growing. Your preparation and hard work has become a source of strength for the final task. Only in retrospect will you know how much you have grown and changed—and how thoroughly you are prepared to meet this ultimate challenge.

It is now time for your loved one to die...and you have done everything within your power to be ready. You have arranged a quiet, soothing environment, and now family, friends, religious or spiritual advisors, and perhaps the caregivers may all be gathered. You may all be at home, in the hospital, in a residential facility, or in a hospice house. Your loved one has come to terms with his life as best he can and is as prepared as he can be for the pending event. Those present have also accepted the death of this person.

Only in looking back, can we see clearly how completely things unfolded and how well you all played your parts. The partnership that you have established provides the framework that will facilitate the transition to death. You and the other caregivers are all working together, providing the bridge from life to death.

This is also the time at which you can understand even more about the dying process by learning about what happens to the physical body during the last days and moments of life. Although it may sound clinical, there is science in dying. It's important to understand this, because it can help you prepare for things that could be uncomfortable at times, and it will help to make your loved one's transition easier to endure. By knowing what to expect during the physical change from life to death, you will feel more able to cope with the things over which you have absolutely no control.

There may be a surge in energy. Your dying loved one may even ask for a favorite food. The mood may lighten, and he may want to see friends and relatives he hasn't seen for a long time. It is likely that the spiritual energy needed for transition is being harnessed, and a synchronistic event may be near. The spiritual energy is physically exerted to accomplish this final task.

Physiologic Death: What Happens When Your Loved One Dies

Exalt, oh shores and ring, oh bells

but I with mournful, tread

walk the deck my captain lies

fallen cold and dead.

—*Walt Whitman*

Throughout the ages, people have assigned death its meaning in accordance with their beliefs, customs, and cultures. The Greeks saw death as a journey across the river Styx, and in some cases, a dark pilgrimage into the underground. Native Americans speak reverently of a return to the Great Spirit of the Grandfather and the Grandmother. Christians see death as a step in a joyous reunion with God. Buddhists speak of the cycle of rebirth and of becoming one with the universe. Yet death is an event that happens, not only to our souls, but also to our bodies. And all people seem to agree that before a soul can be freed to transcend or migrate or rejoin its creator, the vessel for the soul—the body—must endure a physiologic event from which it does not recover.

It is important, therefore, to have a rudimentary understanding of how the physical body sustains life, and ultimately relinquishes it. The entire dying process is a complex biochemical cascade of movement, color, and sound, which we are now able to observe and begin to understand.

The process of respiration is what makes energy so the cells and body can carry out their work. In essence, respiration keeps us alive. This dynamic occurs in every cell of the body, nurturing and sustaining tissues and organs. The organs are specialized, enabling us to eat, drink, feel, smell, taste, move, react, talk, interact with others, and reproduce. When cellular respiration slows down, it begins with the tiniest cell, then advances to tissues and organs. When breathing stops, there is no more oxygen available for the business of cellular respiration, or making energy. Once there is no more respiration (both in the cells and breathing), our most basic interaction with the world—the simple exchange of gases—ceases, and the brain and body dies.

The body shuts down in a preferential fashion because there is a built-in mechanism to protect certain vital organs. The heart, brain, and kidneys, for example, are protected for a brief time before they shut down and can no longer function. When breathing stops, the brain is deprived of oxygen and the energy necessary for its functions. That's when your loved one is said to have died. The brain no longer thinks, makes decisions, perceives and directs the body or allows the person to live. Brain death, as it's called, allows us all to go to sleep naturally and painlessly after breathing stops. In this way, nature has devised a beautiful way for us to doze off into eternity peacefully and painlessly.

As the brain dies, it no longer transmits impulses or controlling messages, and consequently, the temperature control mechanism also stops. As the body cools, there is no longer warm blood flowing through the arteries and veins. Sometimes the nerves and the heart continue to function after the patient has been "dead" for several minutes, but this too stops and shuts down quickly.

At this point, all life processes have stopped. There is no longer an ability to taste, feel, see, speak, breathe, make waste, eat, metabolize food, or make energy. The body, which once housed a person, is empty of what we think of as *life*. It is as inanimate as the bed upon which it rests. The body, which your loved one's soul occupied, is dead.

One evening, Pam was strolling with a friend through the Fisherman's Wharf area of San Francisco. This neighborhood is famous for its fresh seafood, its tourist attractions, and its bright city lights. As they were walking under a large and somewhat garish marquee, the electricity began to fail. The effect was subtle at first, but soon thousands of little lights began to flicker and dim. Soon individual letters were flashing and fading. The color patterns that kept the letters connected, forming words and images, started to lose their intensity. The letters became fragmented and unreadable. Starved of electricity, the sign blinked on and off in an irregular pattern for a few seconds, until finally it was blank, dark and still.

Pam's friend, as much an artist as a biochemist, looked at her and smiled, a little sadly. "That's death," he said. "That is how everything dies. From electrical signs to supernovas."

He was right. First the small lights—bulbs, cells, or stars—lose their electrical charge and warmth. Then everything that organizes around them, of which they are a part—letters, kidneys, or planets—dies off. Soon the stuff that holds everything together begins to unravel, and death comes to the whole—the whole sign, the body, or the universe. And so it is.

What, then, can we expect at this moment of transition? Death has likely been occurring for several weeks, and many events have transpired. Death comes in its own way, on its own time. The dying loved one may be disoriented, asleep, or resting quietly. This may be described as "having one foot in each world."

Your loved one may talk to the gathered family, friends, and caregivers about places and events unknown to anyone else. Or the focus may be in the present physical world. He may see or feel those he has loved that preceded him in death, or he may converse with someone from his secret life. He may be agitated, picking at the bedding or throwing it off. It's common that physical activity is aimless and movements appear random. As death draws near, he may exhibit increased restlessness due to lack of oxygen. Breathing becomes sporadic, stopping for a minute, only to start up again just as suddenly. The breathing will probably be shallow and from the mouth.

Changes in breathing during the active dying process can be dramatic. Be prepared to hear puffing, snoring, and halted breathing. This cycle may repeat itself many times. All the while, your loved one may be pursing his lips. There may also be a cough or a congested gurgling sound. This is caused from fluids or saliva pooling in the trachea (breathing tube) or the lungs. This is known as the "death rattle," although it may not necessarily indicate that death is imminent, since breathing could return to normal in the next minute. If his breathing is too loud, gently reposition him by placing pillows under him to lift up the chest and head.

Helping Your Loved One with the Physical Symptoms of Dying

What can you do if your loved one gasps for air? As people die, they often develop a loud breathing pattern. Your loved one will continue this pattern, possibly until death. His breath may also become very shallow and very irregular. There may be longer and longer periods between breaths. This can be difficult for you to observe and to hear. Usually your loved one is unaware of his breathing and of your distress because of it. If he seems to be suffering, struggling, or displaying any symptoms of air hunger, ask your hospice nurse about beginning or increasing his Roxanol or Ativan. Either of these medications will help his breathing to relax.

If his mouth is dry, use sponge swabs to moisten his lips and tongue. Some ice chips may be offered if he is alert enough. Be very careful with giving liquids, as he may not be able to swallow. Simply stroke his forehead so he can feel your presence. Your loved one may be incontinent now, both of stool and urine. Because his intake of food and fluids has decreased as illness has progressed, there may be much less bodily waste.

There are adult diapers and waterproof disposable bed pads that can be of help in caring for him. Be sure to keep your loved one clean and dry and to use lotion and powder on his skin to prevent irritation.

Your loved one's nose may run, and there may be some drool from his mouth. Just wipe it away.

Some people have a desire to actually climb into bed with their dying loved one and cradle him as he leaves. This is a very loving act. It is also very individual, and you should not do anything that makes you uncomfortable.

Sharing the Final Days

When people are dying, they are busy with the act of disengaging. It is often difficult to distinguish between the need to provide comfort and giving into the desire that he change his mind and not leave. You will have to listen to your own heart on this one.

There are some things you can do to be as supportive as possible during your last days together:

- Talk with him about special times you have known together.

- Play his favorite music, or music that has a special meaning to you both.

- Remind him of the difference he has made in life.

- Be sure he knows that those he leaves will take care of each other.

During these last weeks, days, or moments, facial muscles are often relaxed, and the jaw is slack. You'll notice his eyes are often half-open and unfocused. Sometimes there will be a response to verbal interaction, but this diminishes as death approaches. His temperature may fluctuate from hot to cold, accompanied by increased sweating or clamminess. His skin color will change with the variances in body temperature or loss of circulation. The skin can appear pale or have a dull yellowish tint. His nail beds and feet may be bluish because of dwindling circulation. His blood pressure may be low, and his pulse could be fast, or so slow as to be imperceptible.

It may help you to know that, at this stage, there is typically no pain or discomfort. Mother Nature apparently provides an internal analgesia that's released as death approaches. This analgesia is often sufficient to keep the individual totally pain-free. If, however, you detect discomfort from the disease itself or an existing injury, feel free to ask for medications to promote comfort and mitigate anxiety.

The focus of your loved one's remaining energy is literally changing from being a life force in this reality to detaching from it and preparing for the next. You can reassure him that you will make this transition as comfortable and pain-free as possible. To do this, ask that the hospice care team be on duty with an emergency pain pack available. This is the package of medications that the hospice nurse left in your home during one of her earlier visits. She told you that you could call hospice in the event of any pain emergency, and they would tell you exactly how to administer this medication. Typically, there will be a liquid form of morphine called Roxanol. You will be told how to place a drop or two into your loved one's mouth, between his gums and cheek or underneath the tongue. He does not have to swallow it. The medicine will be absorbed through the skin of his mouth. There may also be some Ativan or other tranquilizer in the pack. This is to treat any accompanying anxiety. Sometimes what appears to be pain may, in reality, be fear. In those cases, Ativan or a similar medication will be more effective than morphine.

Having carefully attended to his physical needs, you can now devote yourself to the psychological and spiritual needs of both your loved one and yourself. Talk softly with him. Use gentle words of encouragement and confirm that focusing on love will make the transition easier. Emphasize the good things your loved one has done during his life and on this difficult journey to death. Tell him that although you will miss him and go through a period of mourning, you and other family members will take good care of each other. The dying are greatly comforted by reassurances of this kind. Give him permission to leave as you offer him your love, gratitude, and blessings.

Even if he is unresponsive, presume that he can hear your words and that he is profoundly comforted by your presence.

At this juncture, we'd like to stress what else is going on. As you now know, the dying process comprises biological change. Your loved one's psychological journey is, in part, an attempt to accommodate the transformations occurring within his body. Whatever course the disease has taken, whatever discomfort your loved one has experienced, this is the point at which pain is virtually exclusively borne by those who love and are with the person who is dying. You have gone through an enormously demanding season to get to this point. If you have allowed yourself to share in your loved one's burden, then you can now appreciate that you, too, are at a crucial point of transition.

Saying Goodbye with a Knowing Compassion

We believe that an individual can sense when the end of his life is near. He may signal it to you in ways that you'll understand only in retrospect. In fact, your loved one may not even be aware that he is sending the message. This can be tough stuff—hard to decipher, hard to understand, and hard to accept. When your dying loved one is signaling to you that "this is it: I am dying," then the last stage of life is before you. It's no longer the beginning or middle of the end: it's the end of the end.

Sometimes the message is crystal clear, but sometimes it's garbled because your loved one is weak, groggy, or can only speak in whispers. Sometimes the message is unspoken and delivered through a physical signal, such as a hand squeeze, or a last hug or smile. We encourage you to be aware of all of the possibilities, and to be open to this moment.

It is a big moment indeed. This is when it's time to say "Goodbye," "I love you," or "We will see you again." Again, reassure him that he is loved and that he will not be forgotten. Grant any last wish or desire, and assure him that the wish will be carried out. This is your last opportunity to thank him for being part of your life, no matter how short your involvement has been. Be open. Let your mind, and the emotion of the moment, guide you on what to say or do. Remember Rilke's *unknowing*. Go into your own unknowing. Trust that if it comes from love, whatever you do or say will be okay.

Compassion, in the dying moments, is perhaps the greatest gift you can bestow on your loved one. Byock suggests that in order to do this, you must conjure up an image of what you think your loved one is going through and what you feel he needs you to do at any given moment, and then do it. This is a highly intuitive experience. To succeed, you must totally clear your mind and be receptive to an "imaginative alignment" with your loved one. But it does require a willingness on your part to share the pain with your loved one. In that exquisite and painful sharing, you communicate genuine compassion to him, and ultimately, ease his transition. Indeed, the inherent power of this experience can be transformational for each of you.

In the moments before your loved one dies, the physiological process continues, and carbon dioxide builds up in the blood, allowing the body to relax and relinquish the soul into eternity. Ultimately, your dying loved one withdraws completely into a semi-conscious, somnolent state. And finally, he is gone.

Stan

Stan was a beloved family doctor who had practiced in the same community for over forty-five years. He had many loving patients, and practiced in the traditional role of the old-time family doctor. He was also a retired soldier and a survivor of the Bataan Death March.

When Stan retired at the age of seventy-eight, it was a huge event in his community, and he was sent off with a big celebration, and lots of love and tears. He had lived a wonderful life. People admired and adored him. He had done well financially and was surrounded by a devoted family.

Stan had not been ill a day in his life, but during the second year of his retirement, he felt a sudden shortness of breath and a hunger for air. An X-ray revealed that both lungs were filled with tumors. Surgery was not an option, nor was any other kind of treatment. The prognosis was not good. So, heroically and mindfully, Stan prepared to die.

Stan's family was close at hand throughout all of his preparations—everyone except his daughter, Julie. She had left on an extended trip to Europe prior to Stan's diagnosis, and efforts to contact her were unsuccessful. Even so, Stan vowed he would not die until he saw her one last time.

As soon as Julie returned home, she got word of her father's rapidly declining health and quickly found her way to his side. By the time she arrived, Stan was approaching death. He was using oxygen and taking morphine for pain and anxiety. It was a tearful reunion. After spending several hours alone with his beloved daughter, Stan announced, "Now I have to go."

Everyone thought this to mean that he had to urinate, and all but Julie went searching for a receptacle. When they came back to the room, Stan was gone. Julie was holding his hand.

Life After Your Loved One's Death

It's finally over. Your loved one has relinquished his body. You are left with finishing the processes of this long, intense season.

If your loved one is a hospice patient, call the hospice agency if they are not already there. They will send a nurse to your home to verify death. If you are not affiliated with hospice, call your primary care doctor. If you are in a hospital, skilled nursing facility, or hospice house, the pronouncement will be done as a matter of protocol.

Your hospice nurse or social worker will probably stay with you until the mortician arrives and picks up the body. Of course, you can request to be alone with your loved one until that happens. The amount of time you spend with the body is determined by your set of beliefs (*i.e.*, you may have a religious or spiritual ritual to perform). If you want more time to say good-bye, make peace, bathe the body or perform a ritual, you do have the option to call the mortician later. But the body should be picked up within twelve hours so that it can be prepared for viewing and burial, in accordance with your plans and customs.

You will be offered grief counseling and support immediately after your loved one's death. You can take advantage of it right away or in the future, depending on your needs. Hospice agencies generally offer grief support and emotional support for at least a year following death.

This can take the form of telephone contact on important dates, individual grief counseling, and bereavement support groups. Most bereavement groups are offered to the entire community. You do not need to be a hospice client to participate in the bereavement groups.

Remember that you do not *have* to be alone. Your religious advisor or clergyman can be of great help and comfort. Let your friends and peripheral families—church, school, clubs, work, social groups, veterans' groups, etc.—take an active hand in helping you in this hour of need. You will need both privacy and companionship. The others in your life have also suffered this loss. They may need you, too, more than you know.

You may need to see your accountant or lawyer to assist with any remaining financial issues. Contact your insurance agent and inform her of your need for expeditious payment on life insurance policies. This is the time to put into effect the plan you and your loved one worked out when he was still cogent. If your loved one was a veteran, you may be eligible for benefits. Contact the Department of Veterans Affairs or a local veterans' organization to learn more.

If you do not have prearranged funeral plans, these arrangements will have to be made now. If you had an opportunity to talk with your loved one about funeral plans, you will know if he wanted a modest memorial service at home or a more elaborate funeral. Even if you didn't have a specific conversation about final arrangements, you know what his beliefs and values were. You may be emotionally vulnerable at this time, and there could be a temptation to spend more money than you can afford—and more money than your loved one would want you to spend. It is often a good idea to bring a friend with you to the mortuary.

Or get help from those who have been by your side all along. They, too, love you and your departed loved one, and their presence will bring you comfort and perhaps some calm at this vulnerable time. Some hospice organizations have financial and business advisors who can help you in this time of need.

Funerals and memorial services are not for the departed. They are for the living. They are forums that allow you to express your love for the one you have lost, and for you to receive the love and support of your family, friends, and community. A memorial service need not be an expensive, elaborate undertaking. If your loved one was buried quickly and quietly or cremated, you can have an informal gathering in your home or church. You do not need to prepare a eulogy, although you may certainly wish to. Family and friends can be invited to share their memories of the departed one. It is in sharing your grief and love with others that healing happens.

Funeral arrangements are not always made prior to an expected death. More often, they are made at the deathbed or just after the death. In some cultures, it is considered disrespectful to make arrangements prior to the death; doing so suggests a lack of love. Other cultures don't need to plan; they *know* what they will do because their burial customs are so ingrained in tradition that there are no decisions to be made. Making funeral arrangements prior to death—especially with the participation of the dying person—is a very new concept. It is almost exclusively a western custom.

References and Reading

Karnes, Barbara, <u>Gone From My Sight: The Dying Experiences</u>, Stillwell, Kansas, 1986.

Byock, Ira, "When Suffering Persists," *Journal of Palliative Care,* Vol. 10, No. 2, pp. 8–13, 1994.

8

THE DEATH OF A CHILD

The little toy dog is covered with dust

but sturdy and staunch he stands

And the little toy soldier is red with rust

and his musket molds in his hands

Little Boy Blue

—*Eugene Field*

When a child dies, those who loved her experience an unparalleled tragedy. The emptiness that surrounds the places where she once lived and is no longer present is a heavy emptiness. It's as though something essential has been sliced out of the air. A fundamental piece of love and life has vanished, and it is therefore a unique emptiness.

When the life and presence of a child is gone, so are the many qualities the child brought into the lives that she occupied or touched. Children fill our lives with special things, and when they are gone, the essence of them cannot be replaced. For instance, the innocent laughter at what adults don't see as funny (but which actually is funny); their particular interpretation of what adults may consider mundane; their observations and wonder at the newness of everything. Indeed, everything *is* new to a child. Although some adults don't understand it, part of what's magical about children is their countless questions, bizarre answers, and the unique perceptions they hold as true.

There are some universal axioms that we teach our children: God is good; Allah is great; you must have pity on people who have less than you; your love will be returned; good will triumph over evil; and so on. These all help to build the child's faith and belief in humanity, but not necessarily in reality. They are true nevertheless.

Adults tend to believe that the death of a child is premature, that the child didn't live long enough to understand life, to live life, to experience all the joys and wonder this world has to offer. Some people believe the death of a child is innocence betrayed. We wonder if perhaps the innocent love and trusting nature of children helps in the soul's transition.

When a couple chooses to have a child and make her part of their lives, they think of the child as belonging to them—not to the cosmos, with its own rules and timing. They expect their child will be happy and healthy, grow old, and most certainly outlive them. Surely, there are fears that surface—deeper fears than ever experienced before the birth of the child—but no parent is prepared to deal with the actual death of their child. This is in part why they grieve so deeply.

In our work, we've also witnessed that parents often feel badly because they weren't able to prepare their child's young soul for the transition to death. After all, childhood is too early a time to talk of death and accepting mortality. Even if people don't consciously know how they would prepare their offspring for the fact that we all die, parents want to feel that they have done whatever they can.

When a child dies, many parents feel cheated because a fundamental process was not complete, and they were unable to adequately attend to their child's soul. We want to remind you that the child who has just died has lived a full life! His life was likely more intense than that of other children, and his life has accomplished what it was created for, however short or long.

There are so many questions and thoughts that barrage parents who lose their children—all wedded to deeply intense emotions. It is a horrible shock that leaves loved ones reeling.

Parents, friends, and family members that loved the child therefore carry a heavier burden of guilt than they can often bear. It's no wonder: add guilt to the suffering and sadness they feel, and it's a truly extraordinary kind of grieving that requires particular understanding and support.

We urge parents to recognize that they have done nothing *wrong* in their parenting. Loving their child and bringing him or her up in the way they thought best is what parents are supposed to do—and is all they can do. Cloaking the loss in guilt makes the suffering so much worse.

We believe the shock of a child's death is felt not only by the living, but also by the souls of those who are awaiting her. In essence, the sadness is also felt on the other side of the log bridge.

Sometimes it may seem like all of creation is witness and partner to your pain. The clouds well with tears until the entire sky bursts and rages against this inconceivable loss. The night sounds of crickets and frogs seem to chant a mourner's Kaddish all night long. And the sun can burn angrily on even the mildest spring mornings.

If it seems to you like the death of your child has diminished the light and joy of the world, we believe that it is true. The burden of your grief is shared by all of creation. The enormous hole in your world is also felt elsewhere. But we also believe that your child will be guided to wherever the precious souls of children dwell, and that she will be welcomed with love and joy. Whatever your spiritual beliefs, work on knowing that your child is finally safe where pain cannot touch her.

In "Medical Care of the Soul" (Johnson Printing, Boulder, Colorado, 2000) Bruce Bartlow explains what we mean by this. He refers to the beliefs of the Central African shaman: a child bonds easily with elders from her family because she has just come from the spiritual world with news for the grandparents, who are nearing the end of their physical life here on earth. The shaman believes that those nearest to the spiritual world (the young and the old) can communicate well with each other because of their mutual nearness to the spiritual world. The child remembers her recent journey from the spiritual world to the physical world, and can easily find her way back to reconnect with her ancestors. This can be a comforting notion when groping for peace of mind after the loss of a child.

Generational Imperative

Death has happened to children forever. Like everyone born before them, children sign up for the basic truth that everyone dies. And like adults, children also become ill, they are in terrible accidents, and they can die suddenly and unexpectedly. The cause of death doesn't matter. Every time the innocence and joy children bring into the world is diminished by death, pain and sadness runs very deep.

The loss of an adult child is just as painful and soul-wrenching as the loss of a young child. The death of a child of any age goes against what we call the "generational imperative." Parents, aunts and uncles, grandparents, granduncles and grandaunts have collectively, albeit unconsciously, decided that they must all die before their children. This seems to be the right way, and feels natural. Anything contrary to this imperative is an inviolable taboo—regardless of the child's age. The loss of a child, at any age, releases unbridled grief.

Parents with a child that comes close to death but survives will feel this same grief until the child is no longer in danger. Cases where a child comes close to death several times, but continues to be saved, create incredible turmoil. These parents face many moments of soul-searching and self-blaming, but somehow manage to bond stronger with the child. Bonds are stronger from having endured these harrowing experiences.

It is the same with the special bonds between parents of special-needs children, for example, those with Down's syndrome, cerebral palsy, cystic fibrosis, and many of the mental and central nervous system anomalies.

In these cases, the parents feel a unique love for those disadvantaged children, and the child's death leads to incredible emotional turmoil. Suffice it to say, we feel the pain and sorrow of all parents who lose children to illness or other tragedies.

After the Child's Death

Once the child has died, the effect on family and siblings can be devastating. Parents can drift apart, creating deep separation. Siblings may not express their sorrow in ways that adults expect them to, and their behavior can become problematic. After a child's death, family dynamics are difficult to predict, and very complex to understand. The prescription calls for lots of love, understanding, and strong support. We recommend calling hospice, getting into a grief-busting program, or seeking help from a professional counselor. For many people, the grieving remains very intense and there is a need to participate in therapy for years. Some people don't fully realize their grief until long after the child dies. Healing from this kind of loss is an ongoing process without a linear path or a straight and narrow set of rules clarifying when the pain should be complete. The most important thing to do is to stay true to what you're experiencing, and to deal with it in the most constructive manner possible. This will most likely require help from other people.

Religion can play a huge part in helping to deal with this special grief. The family's time with a child can end abruptly, leaving them with overwhelming feelings of emptiness and incompleteness. Still, it's important to acknowledge that the child's life was a complete cycle, however short that cycle may have been. Synchronicity can be present even in a tragically shortened life.

The strong emotional ties rooted in the generational imperative often prevent parents from perceiving the beauty of synchronicity at play in the family dynamic. With tears in our eyes, we tell the story of Felicita and her father, who could not bear to let go of his daughter.

Felicita

Felicita was a surgical nurse at a local hospital. She was a good mother and a loving wife and well-respected by her colleagues. Her husband was successful in his career, and her children were doing well in school. Life was good, by any yardstick.

Felicita brought her parents up from Mexico, after years of struggling to get their papers in order. Shortly thereafter, she started having vague belly pain and noted some blood in her stool. She went to her doctor for both her annual physical and to get the pain checked out. All of the lab tests were normal. Her mammogram was normal. She did have some mild anemia and a small amount of blood in her stool, so she was referred to a gastroenterologist for further evaluation by a colonoscopy.

On the day of the procedure, she was anxious and felt some foreboding about what the doctor might find during the examination. The exam was completed easily, without problem. But the concerned look on the doctor's face when he came to speak with her caused the blood to drain out of her own face. He had found a large tumor in the transverse colon, and it seemed to be growing through the different layers of the colon. He sent off several biopsies, as well as some lymph nodes from the region.

He told Felicita that she needed to see a surgeon for an open abdominal exploratory surgery and a staging procedure to determine the extent of tumor spread. This was a crucial piece of information, since all therapy, including future surgery, would depend upon the spread of the tumor. Felicita knew what was involved in the staging procedure, having participated in many of these types of operations.

She went home feeling numbed by the day's events. She was in shock, and seemed as though in a trance. She called her husband as soon as she was home and told him that she had been diagnosed with cancer. He started to cry on the phone, and came home immediately. When the children arrived home from school, Felicita and her husband told them everything. Felicita's parents were informed later that evening, and they came over offering hugs, kisses, and support. Her parents slept in the guestroom that night, and took over the kitchen and housekeeping chores.

The exploratory surgery confirmed the fact that the tumor had spread far from the bowel. It occupied much of her abdomen, but had also traveled to her liver and brain. Although this was terrible news, Felicita accepted it, and prepared to die. With composure and clarity, she chose minimal chemotherapy, but heavy palliative care and comfort measures.

Felicita's family was loving and supportive during this process—with the exception of her father. He turned inward and suffered alone. After Felicity came home from the hospital with a feeding tube in her, he told the family that it was not right that a child should die before the parent, no matter what the circumstances. He felt very strongly about this, and refused any further food and sustenance.

The priest could not convince him to change his mind. His wife tried to get him to realize that Felicity needed his support as she battled the cancer, but he would not be convinced.

Eventually, the tumor pinched off Felicita's feeding tube. Once again, she was admitted to the hospital for a bowel bypass operation that would enable her to receive nourishment and reduce the adverse effects of bowel obstruction. But after the operation, she was having a difficult time recovering. Short of breath, she was in and out of coma. Her father came for a visit at this time and saw her struggle to live. He told the nurses in the recovery room that what was happening was not right, that parents should not outlive their children. He then took a cab home while the rest of the family stood by, making sure Felicita would make it. Indeed, she did survive the operation, although she was weak and gravely ill.

Later, when the family returned home, they entered a dark house, and found Felicita's father lying on his bed, lifeless. He had written a note, which said simply, "I love you, my family. It is not right that my child dies before me. I must die before you. I will see you in heaven."

He had come home and willed himself dead. This was how strong his conviction was that children should not die before their parents. Felicita died several weeks later.

Sometimes a child's death is not only untimely, but violent as well. How might you as parents and family react if a loved one dies violently? You might react with anger, by withdrawing from your social circle and family, by losing your faith, or perhaps with personality changes or violent behavior. The effects of violent deaths are profoundly devastating and can change lives dramatically. How could you deal with these events? The story of Uncle Freddie and Tom will show you how one father found his way out of the path of darkness and despair.

Uncle Freddie and Tom

There is a Jewish teaching about the *lamed vav*. *"Lamed vav"* means "thirty-six." The rabbis teach that at every moment on earth there are thirty-six souls *(tzaddikim)* who are so virtuous, so righteous, and so worthy of life that God sustains the entire world for their sake. If not for their existence, we would surely be consumed by our own sinfulness.

The people who knew and loved Tom knew all along that he was a *tzaddik*. His enthusiasm and playfulness won the hearts of our young children. The tenderness he showed his elderly grandmother evoked tears. And in a world where the concept of family is diminished and love for parents goes begging, Tom unashamedly adored his mother and father.

Tom's father, Freddie, was the cantor of a large Reform congregation in Southern California. Tom would often attend Friday night services, which were led by his father. The two men shared a common faith in God and a belief in the goodness of life that bridged their generational and theological differences.

Tom was not quite thirty years old. He was destined to be the hub around which another generation of the family would revolve. As his father had been the center point of the family in our childhood, Tom would be the one to keep the family together, remembering who we were as a people and as a family.

Tom was in the springtime of his life. He had just received his MBA. It was Passover, and he had just returned home from Seder when he was brutally and senselessly murdered during a home-invasion robbery.

Tom's funeral was ceremonious and surreal. It seemed as though everyone in Los Angeles was there, and it felt like the whole world was crying. After the funeral and graveside service, we returned to his parents' home. Tom's great-aunt was telling us that she had been sixty years old when Tom was born. "Who could have known," she asked, "that I would live to see him dead?"

Freddie sat in a high-backed wooden chair. He was gray and silent, staring into space, shaking his head. Freddie had buried his mother just the year before. We sat by his side. This cantor, this man of faith, turned and looked at us with empty eyes. "There is no God," he said quietly. Joyce, Freddie's wife, took his hand and squeezed it. She didn't say anything at all, but her presence was enormous.

Uncle Freddie and Aunt Joyce were soon pulled into the hell of a long and unfathomably painful trial and sentencing for the man who had taken Tom from us. For a while, there were no family celebrations or gatherings. Freddie and Joyce were struggling to pick up some of the pieces of their shattered lives; the rest of us had no heart for celebrating. The normal markers of life (weddings, bar mitzvahs, birthdays) seemed only to take us further and further from a world that included Tom.

In time, family Passovers resumed. They were quieter. And always, there was a hole that could not be filled. Aside from cards at the holidays, we lost touch with Freddie and Joyce. Everyone receded into their own isolated little hell. To have a family gathering without Tom was unthinkable, so over time, we all just stopped trying. Years passed in this disorganized and lonely way. Then, last spring, a family emergency brought us back together again. Freddie's brother-in-law had died, and Freddie was conducting the funeral. We sat over breakfast, discussing the services ahead. I was astonished to hear Freddie speaking again of God, and of the goodness of life. Over the course of fifteen years, Freddie had somehow again found the connection to his life and to his God.

Passover came shortly after Uncle Harry's death. Uncle Freddie again conducted the family Seder. Toward the end of the Seder, the group proclaims, "We and our children will live…the people of Israel will live." Freddie's voice was sure and firm as he made the declaration, "The people of Israel will live." How could he say that, after the loss of his only son and the recent death of his beloved brother-in-law?

On the day of Tom's funeral, Joyce had sat with him, held his hand, and not contradicted him in his desperation and his pain. She had simply been there with him on his journey. Together they had created Tom and nurtured him. Together they had buried him and mourned him. Together they had faced the horror of having lost a child to murder. It was their love for each other that had gotten them through all of this, and that love was the vehicle through which Freddie found his way back to the living world. The hole would always be there, but Freddie had found reason to go on, and he had found meaning in life. He could smile now and tell his famous jokes. And he could make peace with God.

The Legacy

One of the most difficult aspects of losing a child is the sense that there was not a whole life lived. This is seldom the case, as children have an almost magical capacity for living whole lives in a short period of time. But to adults, the time feels cut short. Cut off. And the void left by the loss of a child can make all of life feel hollow and meaningless. Adults have years, seasons, and often children of their own, enabling them to leave an imprint or legacy. Some parents have told us that it eased their anguish to assist in forming and preserving their child's legacy.

Some parents have become advocates and activists about important issues and about circumstances that took their children from them. We all are familiar with the work of Mothers Against Drunk Driving (MADD). Elisabeth Glaser's anguish and outrage at the loss of her child emerged as the Pediatric AIDS Foundation. A family in California whose daughter was murdered worked to pass legislation to keep all our children safer. The law is commonly known as Megan's Law.

Promoting your child's legacy does not have to mean taking on the world—or even the disease that stole her from you. There are many ways parents have found to keep the spirit of their child alive and flourishing in the world and to establish their child's legacy. We suggest some examples:

- Establish a memorial scholarship in your child's name.

- If your child loved music or sports, perhaps your family and/or church community could adopt a sports team or sponsor a children's concert. This could be an annual event.

- If your child loved camping, hiking, or being in the outdoors, create a nature trail through the National Park Service and have a plaque placed in your child's honor.

- Give of your time (when you are emotionally able) to promote your child's special interests: children's theater, dance, art, environmental issues, peace, science fairs—whatever your child loved.

We can't say much more about the enormous grief and heartbreak that parents and other adult family members experience after the death of a child. Each despairing event must be clothed in love and a search for understanding and acknowledgment. Time and love are the great healers of many wounds.

There are some organizations that can help parents with a dying child or the pending transition to death. We only list some of these, and leave it to you to find them in your local area: HAND, Circle of Friends, Candle Lighters, Touchstone, Make a Wish Foundation, Hospice. Your local hospice organizations can also direct you to individual grief counseling and appropriate group therapy.

When Children Lose Their Mom or Dad

And when one of us is gone

and one of us is left to carry on

then remembering will have to do.

Our memories alone will get us through.

Think about the days of me and you

And you and me against the world

—Helen Reddy

One of the most difficult and painful situations is when a parent dies, leaving young children. Children do not have the vocabulary to speak of their pain, fear, and grief. We will use the term "mom," but we are talking of both mom and dad. Please read this with that in mind.

A child's understanding of death is limited, and very different from an adult's. For one thing, young children (generally children younger than six years old) do not comprehend the concept of permanence. They simply have no adequate reference point. Children use words like "death" and "die," but they can't conceptualize "forever." Following a parent's death, the child may ask over and over again, "But when is she coming back?" We remember a four-year-old boy who sat on the back steps day after day, waiting for his mom to return home. Every day his dad would go to him and remind him that Mom had died. And the next day, Michael would be on the back steps again, waiting for his mother.

A child's experience and expression of grief is also different from ours. Children have a limited attention span—and that includes their emotional attention span. A child may not sit and mourn or cry as an adult would. He needs to take a break and play. Children need distraction. For example, when Pam's daughter was twelve years old, her grandmother died on October 30. Sherry was close to her grandmother and was profoundly affected by her death, yet the next night she insisted upon going trick-or-treating. It would be unacceptable for an adult to want to attend a festive event or party the day after the death of a loved one. It's completely normal for children, however.

Don't expect a child to have the vocabulary or insight to talk about her grief. Children identify strongly with physical sensations, especially the physical sensations of distress. Listen for: "My tummy hurts." Children often feel their sadness as tension in their abdomens. Children also say, "My throat hurts," referring to the sensation of holding back their tears. A little girl we know asked for adhesive bandages. Every five or ten minutes, she would come in, point to a place on her little arm or leg, and ask us to put a bandage there. Her father put her on his lap, tended gently to her invisible injuries, and hoped that his love could somehow help her heal the pain she could not articulate. One little girl we worked with during her mother's battle with cancer had no words at all. Jennifer communicated with us through her beautifully expressive and compelling artwork.

Jennifer's Mommy

Grace was well-named. She was kind and loving, with a special gentleness of spirit. She was a young wife and mother with a loving husband and two daughters who adored her. Shortly after the birth of her second daughter, Jennifer, Grace was diagnosed with breast cancer. Grace waged war against the cancer with surgery, radiation, and chemotherapy, and a remission was achieved. Four years later, Grace's cancer recurred.

Grace's older daughter remembered her mom's earlier struggle with cancer, but Jennifer, the five-year-old, had been an infant during Grace's original treatment. To have Mommy away from home and in the hospital was a totally new, terrifying, and heartbreaking venture into the unknown.

I met with Grace many times over the course of her treatment. She suffered debilitating nausea, fatigue, and bouts of peripheral neuropathy from the potent drugs used for "salvage" chemotherapy. Grace's courage and resolve were always bolstered by her children's visits. "My biggest fear," she told me, "is of dying and leaving them. I am so close to my mother. I can't imagine my girls growing up without a mom." Grace's oldest girl was seven, and they would often talk into the afternoon; Angela would bring in her schoolwork to share with Grace. As Grace began to lose ground, Angela increasingly identified with and sought refuge in the love of her grandmother and her father.

It was harder for Jennifer. She would often sit at the foot of the bed, somehow separated from the family circle. Jennifer wasn't articulate like Angela, and often quietly sucked her thumb when Grace and Angela had their mother-daughter talks. Grace tried to draw Jennifer into the conversation, but Jennifer continued to pull away into her own thoughts. Grace was concerned about her youngest daughter, and would often speak with me about this, sometimes seeking advice, sometimes just looking for support. Jennifer was clearly overwhelmed and drowning. Worse: drowning in silence; drowning without a voice.

Our art therapist suggested that we encourage Jennifer to draw pictures of her world. This proved a wonderful medium for releasing Jennifer from her isolation. On the first day, she produced a picture of two little girls crying. In her childish scrawl, she wrote: "My heart is sad...I am sad you are gone and when you get, back I will love you. I love you and I am so sad I want you here."

Several days later, Jennifer made a picture story. Jennifer did her storyboard in comic-book style: six frames, two across, three down. In commercial comic-book fashion, Jennifer had begun to talk to us.

Jennifer's pictures became more detailed and more complete as our work together progressed. She was "speaking" to her mother and to all of us. Jennifer's newly discovered voice allowed her to see herself as more complete and more competent, and as more able to solicit the understanding and love she would need to survive the fast-approaching loss of her mother.

Jennifer taught us the importance of reaching out with whatever skills or capabilities we have. A child's message to us can take many forms, and most of them won't be articulated in any way that resembles adult communication.

It is also important to remember that because the personality of a child is constantly developing, the child will experience the loss of a parent at every stage of growth. It is a continuing ache and longing. It can be eased, but it does not go away.

Talking to a Child Whose Parent has Died

A child is vulnerable—helpless in the world. One of her strongest emotional responses to the death of a parent is stark terror: "What will become of me?" Give immediate and complete reassurance that you will keep her safe. Children do not share the worries that adults carry in their minds. Rather, they want to know where they will sleep tonight, and who will tuck them into bed and listen to their prayers. They want to know that someone is at the helm and that the operational components of their world are going to be predictable. Tell them specifically what will happen: "You're going home with Aunt Jenny tonight. You can sleep in our bed with us. Tomorrow we'll have Cheerios." And tell them you love them.

There are a lot of things you must say to comfort and reassure the child, but there are also some things that we urge you *not* to say. They include phrases like:

- Jesus (or the angels) came and took Mom.
- She just went to sleep.
- She went away (or passed away).
- God wanted her in heaven.
- She's in a better place.

These things may be true in a spiritual and emotional context, but children think very literally.

Rather, tell the child that her mom *died.* She may not know the meaning of the word, but she does need to know that it is far different from taking a trip, going away, or falling asleep. We all want to share religious beliefs with children, as faith traditions are a great source of comfort. But children need to know that *God does not come into bedrooms and take people away.* Children need to know that God isn't in the business of snatching people away while they sleep—or they may suddenly fear that this will happen to them. They must also know that a mommy would not leave her child to go anywhere, no matter how nice it is. Emphasize also that death is nothing like falling asleep.

If the child's parent died after a prolonged illness, remind her of the series of losses and physical changes that the parent had to endure. For instance, you can explain: "Mommy's body didn't work anymore. She couldn't eat or drink, open her eyes, or even sleep and have dreams. She couldn't breathe, and her body died."

You may feel that "death" is a harsh word to use with a child, and the truth is that children do not understand the word. But they need to know that something has happened that is different from their everyday experiences. Otherwise the world around them becomes unpredictable and threatening. Will God come for Daddy too? What if Aunt Jenny goes to sleep and doesn't wake up again? Death, however mysterious and scary, should not be confused with everyday occurrences.

Children grieve in their own ways, as best they can. They do not have the same ability to rationalize or understand as adults, and so their pain and grief is special. Be open to all sorts of behavioral changes in children following the death of a loved one. And there is one thing you *must* do: you *must* continue to love them and tell them that you love them. They need constant reassurance that they will not be abandoned.

Griefbusters is a wonderful group of dedicated professionals and volunteers who can help with a child's grieving process. Most hospices will know about it, or employ programs of their own to assist with the stages a child must endure. Don't ignore the needs of your child, even if they are hard to understand and decipher. Acknowledging that this is the biggest life change possible, you need to allow a child to go through the natural process of grieving in his or her own unique way, and do whatever you can to help with healing.

9

POST-SEASON CONCERNS

Your loved one has died—somebody you had never envisioned your life without. No matter how prepared you thought you were, you could never be ready for the endless, agonizing wait for that last breath that never seemed to come, for the nurse to close his eyes for him, for the warmth to leave his body so quickly, or for the stiffness to settle in so soon. Because every person's death is completely different from another's and because your relationship with that person is unique, no one and nothing can take away the feeling that it was all somehow so different from what you had anticipated. All deaths are different. They are connected only by the commonality of grief.

Sometimes the numbness returns for a brief time. Feelings can be muted as you make your way through funeral arrangements and memorial services. There may be trips to the airport and some chaos in the house as you prepare for out-of-town friends and relatives. Emily Dickinson wrote: "After great pain a formal feeling comes. The feet go round their wooden way..." Sometimes the numbness and the maelstrom of activity are a blessing. They get you through those first days and weeks.

Then the door closes, as the last visitor leaves. The phone calls drop off, and then they may stop altogether. The flowers and cards and chicken casseroles may no longer arrive at the door. Some people still have children to tend to, jobs that are calling them, parents and others to console. Some of you now have to learn to live alone, perhaps for the first time in many years. Everyone is aware of a silent void that seems to stretch endlessly into the future.

The Feelings of Grief

There may be times when you feel so overwhelmed by sadness and despair that you are afraid to cry—afraid that if you start to cry, you will never be able to stop. One woman told us, "If I let go, if I give voice to this grief, I will shatter." Feelings of sadness can overtake you at odd moments. A surge of grief can be triggered by a special song, or the experience of running into an old friend, or a scene from a movie that you associate with the person you lost. And sometimes you will have no idea what triggered the tears: they just sprang unexpectedly from that indwelling lake of grief. Many people do a lot of crying while driving in the car.

There are many aspects of the grieving process that do not feel sad. Sometimes you will feel angry. You may be caught surprised by the depth and heat of your rage. It can spill over unexpectedly in social interactions. It can manifest as impatience with delays in traffic, in lines at the supermarket, in travel arrangements. You feel thwarted, ignored, and dismissed.

Grief and healing take enormous spiritual energy. When you have a physical wound, you are often exhausted because your body is directing its energy to heal the wound. The same is true of grief. You may feel exhausted. You may not be able to go about your daily routine without taking short naps or rest breaks. This is especially true if you are having sleep disturbances at night. Many people suffer insomnia with grief.

These emotions can come and go for a long time. Sometimes, when you are in the grip of an intense emotional response, you may feel that you are back at square one, that you have not made any gains at all. In time, you will realize that these sudden upsurges of feelings, unpredictable and unsettling as they can be, are merely a part of the healing process. Over time, over the course of several months, the feelings will come up less often and will have less emotional bite. You will have many bad days. They will gradually become fewer and further apart. You are not losing ground; you are just on a very rocky path. You will need to realize this, respect the difficulty of the terrain, and be very gentle with yourself.

Some Practical Considerations

It is *all* hard, but some particular parts of the day, some rooms in the home, spark very acute pain. There are no magical techniques to manage these places and times, and not every way of coping will work for every person. Some people have found ways that make the pain more bearable for them.

Meals

If you were used to having certain meals together, just the thought of that meal—or that time of day—can be daunting. Some people deal with it by skipping the meal. Once in a while, that is fine. But try not to get into poor eating patterns to accommodate your grief response. It won't work, and you will only compromise your health. Instead, try making small (or larger) changes in the routine of the meal. If the dining room or kitchen table is just too quiet and empty, try eating your meal on a TV table watching a favorite television show, or just the evening news.

If there is a small, friendly diner in your town, you might want to take one of your daily meals there. Let your heart guide you. Some people need the sounds of people around them and the cheerfulness of a friendly place. For others, the thought of venturing out to a restaurant alone would only exacerbate their feelings of isolation.

Many people just don't have the energy or desire to cook for themselves when a spouse has died. Preparing meals will change. You might want to try the frozen entrees that are on the market, or move to easier fare—sandwiches, large salads, soups.

Sleeping

Many people have told us that sleeping alone is the hardest thing to get used to. The bed feels huge and empty. The sheets are cold on your skin. And often the silence is punctuated by creaking sounds that you never noticed before.

Some people get a new bed almost immediately. Some people cannot imagine a different bed. You don't have to decide immediately what to do about the bed (or anything else, for that matter). You can try sleeping in a guest room or just falling asleep on the couch for a while.

If you are sleeping in the bed you shared with your loved one, you might want to try sleeping on his side of the bed. His scent may still be on his pillow. Nestling against his pillow is often a great source of comfort.

This might also be a good time to reconsider allowing a family pet to sleep with you. They miss him too. A woman we know has been sharing her bed with her husband's favorite hunting dog for several months. Two other dogs lie on the floor on either side of the bed. "They're company for me," she says. "And one of them snores just like Ed used to."

We touched earlier on sleep disturbances. Most people experiencing grief also have some trouble with sleeping. One typical pattern is to go to bed exhausted and fall asleep almost immediately, then wake up within a couple of hours. The syndrome of "up and down all night" can be very debilitating. If you find yourself lying in bed awake, we suggest you get out of bed. Go into the living room and find a magazine or a book, or an old movie on television. Trying to sleep during a bout of insomnia is fruitless and frustrating. Over time, these sleep disturbances may diminish. Until they do, try to catch up by sleeping later in the morning or taking short naps early in the day (not late into the early evening hours).

You might also want to try some of the herbal teas and natural sleep preparations. Be sure to let your physician know if you do this. Herbal preparations are medicine, and your doctor needs to know what you're taking. Your doctor may also prescribe a sleep aid for you for a short period of time.

Friends

Your friends are the people who get you through. They are aware of the circumstances of your life, and they choose to be with you anyway. The care and nurturing from your friends is vital to your emotional recovery. Even more than family, your friends can help you manage the pain of loss. Because your friends may not be as emotionally devastated as you are, they will continue their activity in the world, and their love for you can beckon you back into activities of life as you heal.

It is important to remember that the amount or type of support that friends offer you is *not* a reflection of the amount of love they have for you or their estimation of your worthiness. What your friends bring to you in this terrible, dark time is a reflection of their own strengths and weaknesses.

Some friends show their love and concern with their presence in the worst of times, when you may be feeling least loveable. These are the people who listen as you tell the story over and over, again. These are the people who sit with you in the stony silences. These are the people who nod quietly when you say angry, outrageous, or even hurtful things. These are your foul-weather friends.

Other friends who love you just as dearly may not have the personal capacity to absorb so much pain. They are the people who will accompany you to the movies, who will invite you to dinner, who will play golf with you. They love you and they want to draw you out of your sorrow into happier circumstances.

Some friends pick up your children at school, bring dinner and set it on the front step, or inquire about you when they see others who know you well. It is not lack of love that keeps them at arm's length, it is only the lack of ability to be in this painful environment. It is important that you accept with gratitude and love all the gifts your friends bring to you at this time. They know you are hurting. They want to help. Let them.

Professional Counselors

Many people find that talking with professional grief counselors is helpful. They actually perform many of the same functions as your friends do. They listen, then nod. They have no answers, but they will help you address the questions. The main difference between a professional counselor and a personal friend is that your relationship with a counselor is *all about you.* The counselor will not bring her own problems to the table. It is not a reciprocal relationship. She will never suppose that you should loan her your car because of all the hours she has spent with you. She will never call you in the middle of the night in tears. And you will never have to feel guilty, or wonder if you are wearing out the relationship. It is a professional relationship. It exists solely to address your personal needs. You can go to your counselor's appointment with a sense of "leaving it there," and the confidentiality is assured by professional ethics and law. If you feel that it would be helpful for you to speak with a grief counselor, you can find one in your community through your local hospice agency, hospital, or community services agency. Do not hesitate to avail yourself of these services. Often there is no charge for this help.

The final chapter of a book can remind us that just as there was a beginning, there needs to be an ending. The issues of the one left behind are essentially the same as the one that just left.

Psychologists sometimes use the term "survivor guilt" to describe some of the feelings the surviving partner has when a loved one has died. It occurs, in part, because life itself ultimately beckons you forward. You begin, reluctantly at first, to have experiences and challenges that do not include your loved one.

And life works on you. You grow. You change. You develop other aspects to your personality. Your loved one cannot do this; he is frozen in time. He will always be a part of your life, but he is a static part of your life. As you go forward, your life encompasses him and your time with him. You and your life include him, but you are no longer centered on him. Eventually, he becomes a part of your past. You may feel guilty the first time you laugh after he dies, or when you realize it has been weeks since you last felt sadness. You may feel that you are abandoning him. You always have to abandon a part of your past connection to go forward. And you must go forward. You have no choice. Life calls you forward.

Rest assured that you take your love and your memories into your future. One thing many people do is to "check in" with a loved one from time to time. They talk about the day's events, problems they are having, concerns that they once shared. Some people return to the gravesite to have these conversations. Others do it from their kitchen tables, or while they are driving their car.

Will the Pain Ever Go Away?

No. The pain will always be there. The pain will feel like it's going away, but *you* are what will change. Right now the pain is enormous. It owns and defines you. As you move through this process, the pain (like the memories) will take their place in the landscape of your entire life. You grow around the pain, and in the process of your growth, the pain loses its grip. The pain will be contained, even though it is relevant to a major loss. It will become one part of a whole range of feelings you experience. It will always be there, but it will not always be *all* that is there.

In the midst of your grief, there will be confusing and frustrating practical matters to deal with, such as legal issues, wills, probates, Social Security, and medical bills. Get as much help as you can with them. Work these issues into your life on your own schedule and try to forestall any major decisions for at least one year.

Your psychological and spiritual shifts will also give way to new explorations and connections. Your grief may be so deep that you cannot deal with anything but the painful emotion of what you have just experienced. Additionally, you may face problems with unresolved relationship issues.

We often hear of survivors who die shortly after the death of a mate, as we will see in the story of Mrs. Rodarte. This seems more common than we care to acknowledge. In the following final story that we wish to share with you, you will see powerful emotions at play.

Señor and Señora Rodarte

Señor Rodarte was lying on a small bed in a crowded, airless room. There was a large crucifix above the head of the bed. He was surrounded by his children and grandchildren. Although Señor Rodarte was in a deep, seemingly impenetrable coma, all of his children took a moment at his side to say their good-byes, speaking quietly and reverently to their patriarch. Finally, Señora Rodarte was brought into the room. They had been together for sixty years.

She was a small woman, frail and hunched forward. As her wheelchair was carefully positioned by the head of the bed, one couldn't help noticing the tremor in her hands and in her face. Her voice was low and clear and steady as she began to speak. Her daughter translated for us.

"You said 'Come to this country with me. We won't get caught.' So I come to this country with you. And we don't get caught. You wanted children. For you, I had thirteen children. With you, I buried eight children. You wanted to move to San José. So I move with you to San José. You wanted to work in the fields. So I work with you in the fields. And when you become the field boss, I cook for your men. You wanted to retire. You wanted to come here to Hollister. And I come with you to Hollister."

Señora Rodarte leaned forward, pointing at him with her index finger. "How can you do this now?" she asked. "How can you go away like this and not take me with you?"

Señor Rodarte died quietly in the night. His wife was still sitting next to the head of the bed, still asking him, "How can you leave me like this? How can you go away and not take me with you?"

Two months later, we were again visiting the Rodarte family. This time it was to take Mrs. Rodarte into the hospice program. She was sitting motionless and mute in her chair. Her daughter made us tea, encouraging Mrs. Rodarte to take just one sip. It was useless.

"She just sits there like this all day," Mercedes said sadly. "Since Papa died, she goes nowhere—only to the grave on Sundays."

The family had buried Mr. Rodarte at a small cemetery next to the mission church. They took Mrs. Rodarte to mass on Sundays, and then right to the grave, where she would carefully touch the double headstone, studying his name and her own. "Soon," she would say.

One day, after receiving communion in the tiny room she had shared with him all their lives, Mrs. Rodarte asked to be put to bed. "I need to rest now." Her daughter placed her carefully into the bed and covered her tenderly. Mrs. Rodarte curled up against the pillow where he had laid his head, her arm outstretched across his side of the bed. When Mercedes returned to see if she needed anything, it was apparent that she finally had everything she needed. She had found her way across yet another guarded border to join her beloved husband.

"I felt bad at first that she died alone," said Mercedes. "Then I realized that of course, she hadn't died alone. Papa was there. He showed her the way across the final border and made sure her passage was a safe one."

If you live to be a hundred

I want to live to be a hundred minus one day

So I never have to live without you.

—*Winnie the Pooh*

The Gift of Grieving

Healthy grieving, though difficult and painful, cleanses the emotions and facilitates reinvestment in life. Although everyone experiences grief in a personal and unique way, there is a pattern in the journey through loss. The first year following a death is critical. This bereavement year is recognized by many of the world's major religions. There are traditional ceremonies that are helpful in giving voice to your grief; these ceremonies and traditions may be useful to you. And you may want to create your own personal rituals or ceremonies to express the depths of your sadness, and to affirm the existence of hope.

The tasks of grief include intense life review. They also include all of the stages we spoke of earlier: shock, denial, depression, anger, and acceptance.

The past holds new meaning in light of the loss that has occurred. The importance of the "last Christmas" undergoes a radical change when it becomes the *last* Christmas spent together. The meaning of your fifty-sixth birthday is very different if you're a widow on your fifty-seventh birthday. One cannot go into the future until the past has been justified and is congruent with the present.

The gift of your life together transcends loss. These memories are your inheritance, and they will one day be your legacy.

Epilogue

Notes To and About Physicians
A Final Message from Jerry

In his landmark bestseller, "Love, Medicine, and Miracles," surgeon Bernie Siegel states that for true healing to occur, the caregiver must accompany the patient on the journey. The caregiver must, in fact, join the patient in a necessary "leap of faith." A physician trained primarily in physical science may find himself sorely challenged by this concept. Such a suggestion flies in the face of our training. Additionally, physicians often defend against grief and pain by cultivating friendly but impersonal relationships with patients. How do we manage—how do we *dare*—to establish intimate, even loving relationships with our patients? How do we maintain our emotional equilibrium? How do we maintain enough faith in our own competence to continue practicing medicine, given the magnitude of our losses?

The way in which a physician connects with a patient is, in many ways, a reflection of his personal philosophy and an extension of the qualities he brings to all his relationships, both personal and professional. How we interact with our patients, particularly dying patients, speaks compellingly to what we believe about life. If we see life as a biochemical anomaly, an inconsequential "flash in the universal pan," that same detached, passionless quality will be inherent in all our relationships and it will manifest strongly in our relationship with our patients.

If we see life as a test, with a concrete set of regulations, culminating in a reward or punishment or grade, that quality of judgment will permeate our practice and keep the boundaries separating doctor and patient hard and fixed. If we are able to maintain a sense of reverence, and an ongoing inquisitiveness about the process that unfolds before us, we will find it less difficult to participate in our patients' lives and to facilitate the natural rhythm of their life cycle: their births, their aging process, the inevitable changes in their bodies, and ultimately, their deaths. If we can "stay with our patients" throughout the process, we can remain healers in all circumstances, for all the days of their lives. In doing so, we can begin to heal our own lives.

One can see that these challenges present enough of a barrier to caring, but when you add to them the baggage that physicians often bring to the relationship, it often feels insurmountable. How can a physician meet Siegel's challenge to take that "leap of faith" in view of what we learn as students of medicine?

I entered medical school full of hopes and ideals. Modern medicine seemed to offer a cure for man's ills and the panacea for all human suffering. I wanted to be a healer of human beings. I learned a great deal of physiology and biochemistry in medical school: how the cells react to certain stimuli, what medicines kill bacteria and which agents halt the division of cancer cells. I also learned surgery: how to physically remove disease or rearrange the organs to better sustain life. I am grateful for the education I received—and I trust that many of my patients are grateful for my knowledge that "the hip bone's connected to the thigh bone."

The process of caring for an individual to his or her death, however, would be incomplete without addressing those things I learned in medical school that did not serve my patients or me. There were also many things I was simply not taught, things that were deemed not important. Some of these lessons I have learned on my own and modified over the years, and some I struggle to unlearn.

I entered medical school hoping to heal people, and I was taught to fight death. Death was presented as the enemy to be vanquished: the ultimate enemy of humankind. And the battleground upon which the war was to be waged was the patient.

In my capacity as a hospice medical director, I have seen the devastating effects of inappropriately aggressive treatment on patients and their family. I see eighty-seven-year-old grandmothers who are unable to eat, their intestines destroyed by radiation to stop an untreatable cancer. People whose last days are sacrificed, *thrown in front of a train*, by a physician whose desire to stop death supercedes his judgment and obliterates his compassion. I have learned that, despite all of our medical advances, the mortality rate for every generation remains one hundred percent. The question is not "Can we prevent death?" When we are working with a person whose days are short, the appropriate question should be "Can we facilitate life?"

I also learned in medical school, or somewhere along the way, that the doctor must be *in control*: in control of the outcome of disease and treatment and, to some extent, in control of the patient. Patients with ideas differing from ours were labeled as problematic or noncompliant. It was not unusual for that patient eventually to be considered emotionally unstable, even mentally ill. I know now and accept that patients always have their own ideas, thoughts, and patterns.

I know that my job is to provide the best healing I can for the person that my patient *is*. In order to do that, I must know the patient and have some understanding of the world he or she inhabits. I might think he or she should run ten miles a day, give up fried foods, and quit the high-stress counseling job at the high school. She thinks she runs plenty keeping up with the kids, she will give up oxygen before she gives up Kentucky Fried Chicken, and who the hell am I to talk about quitting high-stress jobs?

It is true that we all make lifestyle choices that impact upon our health. However, understanding the underpinnings of these choices, and respecting the patient's absolute right to self-determination, mitigates feelings of caregiver guilt. Caregiver or physician guilt (at not being able to influence a patient's self-care) often presents as "patient-blaming." Here's an example of what I mean.

Ben and Marjorie

I had taken care of Ben and Marjorie for many years. Ben was a hardworking guy with the proverbial "heart of gold." Marjorie was a homemaker, raising four wonderful daughters. Every year Ben would come to my office for his annual physical, which was required by his employer. Every year I would harangue him about his three-pack-a-day smoking habit. "Yeah, Doc," he would say, "I know, I know. Just sign the form, okay? I got to get back to the garage."

The day finally came when I received the hysterical call from Marjorie. Ben had been coughing for a couple of months; it just wouldn't go away. Now he was coughing up blood.

I met them in the emergency room. The X-rays showed a massive lesion on Ben's right middle lung, which later proved to be a primary small-cell lung cancer, which had already metastasized to Ben's ribs and into his brain.

I remember going into the small conference room to break the news to Ben and his family. Marjorie cried, and one of the daughters became hysterical; another was already showing me an article about shark cartilage she had pulled off the Internet. Ben just sat there, dumbfounded. This is his own damn fault, I thought. Why didn't he listen to me about the smoking? As I watched Ben's family descend into their own private hell, my anger at his lifestyle decisions grew deeper.

What was really going on here? I was feeling guilty because I couldn't control Ben's decisions about his health. I couldn't bear the guilt for what I perceived as my "incompetence" in stopping Ben from smoking. Until I could resolve this guilt/anger/blaming behavior *of my own,* it was very difficult to help Ben absorb the information or to assist him in making treatment decisions.

If I could rewrite the medical texts about death, I would include the concept that people die because it is a pre-condition of life, a contract made at conception. People smoke, and it often shortens their lives. People drink and drive, often shortening their lives and the lives of others. People often make terrible decisions with tragic consequences. And, no matter what decisions we make, no matter how carefully planned or foolhardy our lives are, people die. As caregivers, our job is to walk with them for the entire journey, providing the comfort and healing we are trained to give and have trained ourselves to give.

The leap of faith needed to make the journey with patients was not taught during the many years of post-graduate training in which I immersed myself following medical school. I emerged from these programs equipped with the latest and best in technical, objective, and scientific knowledge. I was "loaded for bear" and raring to save lives. I knew that to heal patients and to defeat disease was good, and that to lose in that effort was bad. To some extent, I still subscribe to that theory, but to project that model onto the care of people with terminal illnesses is neither helpful nor appropriate. I saw a patient's death not as a natural passage, but as a failure. Looking at that now, the egotism itself is embarrassingly apparent. The meaning, indeed the ownership, of the patient's death was usurped by my *personal* considerations. In seeing the death of a patient as my failure, I imposed my meaning on this life event. I wanted to take ownership of the patient's death so that I wouldn't fail.

The death of a patient, no matter how inevitable, no matter how appropriate, becomes an event over which doctors flog themselves. We do this privately, and publicly at great staged events called "morbidity and mortality grand rounds." Doctors even study published cases where *everything* is done perfectly, just so they can compare patient-management techniques. The guilt of failure just continues to grow.

Physicians and caregivers face a great number of personal challenges that they need to overcome in order to give the dying patients what they need. The "baggage" that is brought to this relationship must be dealt with and put down, so that physicians and patients can deal with the challenge at hand. The baggage may be from earlier experiences and prior lives. It is no small feat to overcome all of this and become the partner in the final journey.

To succeed, many physicians feel that they must be in control—of the patient, the diagnosis, the treatment, and the lifestyle of the patient. As we discussed earlier, the patient has seniority and control in his or her own life, and will decide whether to get the prescription filled, the blood drawn, or get the x-ray done. After all, barium does not taste good, nor is it comfortable in the "coffin" for the MRI that the physician ordered.

The outcome of the therapy may therefore not be what is anticipated. It can even be disastrous.

The caregiver or physician has to create an environment in which the patient can be treated appropriately, and the patient has to guide the physician or caregiver to help in establishing that environment. This is even more critical if the patient has a terminal illness. The sense of powerlessness the physician has must be acknowledged, expressed—if only to himself—and put aside. It is the patient who is truly in charge. It is, after all, the patient's disease and death.

These are powerful changes in our ways of thinking and interacting, made even more difficult because they entail modifications in our behavior as physicians. Each time we completely and successfully address the impediments we bring to the doctor-patient relationship, a little of this baggage is diminished, enabling the doctor to *be there* for his patient.

Fear of losing a patient, when not acknowledged and processed, can result in a doctor distancing himself from a dying patient. It is so easy for a doctor to hide from a patent behind his clinical white coat. The uniform itself sets the doctor apart. It establishes his identity as a clinician as opposed to a friend.

More often than not, the patient is also in uniform: she is wearing an uncomfortable, revealing examination gown that identifies her immediately as the vulnerable one, struggling to maintain a little modesty, a little feeling of dignity and respectability. One can only wonder how things would feel if we were *all* wearing our pajamas. The visual barriers between doctors and their patients are very powerful. They include massive desks, which infer a hierarchy of importance, with the doctor unreachably high. Some desks are so large that they could place the doctor and his patient in different zip codes! This sets up the illusion of a great (and often unbridgeable) gap between the doctor and the patient and the family. To the extent that a doctor holds his patient at arm's length, to the extent that the doctor sees patients as *them*—to that exact extent, the doctor's ability to be a caregiver and healer is diminished. It is in drawing closer to the patient that both their roles are dignified and validated.

Doctors who cannot tolerate losing a patient sometimes may simply refer them out. There are physicians who, according to their own statistics, "never lose a patient." I wonder if these doctors realize that their dismissal of patients causes anguish to people who have come to trust and rely upon them. I wonder if they know about the incredibly powerful potential they have to facilitate healing, even in the most desperate of situations.

Lisa and Dr. Rogers

The ambulance roared into the hospital parking area, carrying a two-year-old girl who had seized and suffered full arrest while playing Barbie with her mother. The emergency room team worked on Lisa for almost two hours. They were unable to bring her back. As the team had been desperately trying to save Lisa, her large and loving family had assembled in the chapel. The family pastor was with them. They were holding each other's hands and praying when the doctor approached the door. He told them as gently as he could that their precious daughter was dead.

Lisa was wrapped in blankets, and her mother was brought into the trauma room. There was a wooden rocking chair placed by the gurney so that Mom could hold her and rock her on her way.

Mom hummed a lullaby interspersed with sobs. She unwrapped her just enough to count all the fingers and toes. She stroked Lisa's hair. Then she looked at the social worker and said, "Can you get Dr. Rogers? He's our family doctor. He'll know what to do. I need him to tell me she's gone." It was late on a Sunday afternoon. Dr. Rogers was not on call that day, and although he had been their family practitioner for over twenty years, the doctor was preparing for his own retirement. The emergency room physician called Dr. Rogers and explained the situation. He told Dr. Rogers that the child had already been pronounced dead, that there was really no medical need for him to come. He came anyway.

When he arrived, Dr. Rogers approached Lisa, nestled in her mother's lap. He sighed, put a hand on Mom's shoulder, and asked the nurse for a stethoscope. He listened to Lisa's chest. He took Lisa's pulse. He reached out and stroked Lisa's hair. Then he knelt down to speak with her mother, eye to eye. "She's gone," he said quietly. "She's really gone."

Because this family trusted their doctor, his words were able to penetrate the horror and disbelief. The grief and the anguish, and ultimately the healing could now begin. Mom was finally able to relinquish Lisa's body to the coroner.

It is sometimes tempting for a doctor to address the death of a patient in terms of clinical or statistical relevance. Doctors are taught to be objective. And objectivity is, in itself, not a negative quality.

The problem is that people are not objects. And their deaths, like their lives, have profound emotional impact on those who know and care for them. Perhaps the major problem with the statistical response is that doctors can become very good at it—so good that they can become wooden and unapproachable: to their patients, to their loved ones, even to themselves. I have learned, through many years in the practice of medicine, that allowing one's heart to be silent is the ultimate brutality.

God has given you a spirit with wings

to soar to that spacious firmament

of love and freedom.

Is it not pitiful, then, that you clip your wings

with your own hands

and suffer your soul

to crawl like an insect upon the earth.

—*Kalil Gibran, "The Prophet"*

Guilt can cause people once dedicated to healing mankind to turn a deaf ear and a blind eye to the suffering of their patients. For many of us, it is also fear, perhaps fear of our own deaths or fear of losing someone we love. It feels safer to think of death in abstract terms—as an outcome, rather than as a day and an hour and a minute. This fear, this denial, is clearly reflected in our professional verbiage. Patients don't die, they "expire," like a driver's license. It isn't the concept of death that I fear. I am afraid of the day I must sit beside the deathbed of someone I dearly love, someone without whom I cannot envision my life continuing. It is the knowledge that death is not an abstract. It is not a concept. Death is personal. It has a time and a place and a name. And its name is my own. I am not immortal.

As a professional who deals with the most intimate details of people's lives as well as all of the wonderful nurturing caregivers such as you, it is critically important that you summon the courage to look deeply into your own relationships and your own motivations.

You must be willing to address the disappointments, losses, and traumas in your own life. You must appreciate and understand your own yearnings, even those that have remained unfulfilled. These are the pieces of life that influence your ability to be with people in their time of fear and chaos. You have to stay with them, even when it's painful. It is your intimate and thorough understanding of your own "baggage" that allows you to draw upon your past when it's helpful, and to know how to set it aside when it isn't.

Come to the edge.

No, we will fall.

Come to the edge.

No, we will fall.

They came to the edge.

He pushed them, and they flew.

—*Guillaume Apollinaire*

I have learned, through my experience with dying patients, that our willingness to address and explore these great issues of the heart enables us to take that leap of faith. We discover the potential for love and healing in the continuum of life and death and, in doing so, we begin to learn the meaning of both.

References and Readings:

W. Gibson, in <u>Story Poems: An Anthology of Narrative Verse</u>, selected and edited by Louis Untermeyer, Washington Square Press, Inc., 1962.

Bernie S. Siegel, MD, <u>Love, Medicine, and Miracles</u>, Harper and Row, New York, 1986.

R. M. Rilke, <u>Selected Poems of Rainer Maria Rilke</u>, translation by Bly, Harper and Row, 1986.

Patrick W. Flanigan, MD, <u>Surviving the Storm</u>, Pacific Grove Publishing, 1998.

Dick, Lois Chapman, in <u>Living With Grief After Sudden Loss</u>, K. J. Doka, PhD, editor; Taylor & Francis Pubs., March, 1996.

Epilogue

A Final Message from Pam

In 1992, I received a postcard from the University of California San Francisco Medical Center's "Art for Recovery" program. I was so taken by the simplicity and beauty of both the drawing and the poem that I had it framed and have always hung it in my office.

It reminds me daily of who I am and why I do this work. When I called Cindy Perlis, the director of Art for Recovery, for permission to include this picture in the book, I also asked her to tell me a little more about the artist who created it.

"S" was a Buddhist monk. He was a deeply spiritual man who touched the hearts and lives of all his caregivers at UCSF. Cindy tells me, "I would walk into his room and everything changed. Even the air was different." At first, "S" resisted Cindy's encouragement to participate in the art program, stating that he could not draw, that he had no talent. Cindy persisted. One day she asked him to draw a picture of his spirit. And the following picture is what "S" drew.

And so we complete our circle of time with each other and with you. The same energy that brought you to this book fanned our need to write it. In the same manner that you are connected to your loved one, so are we all connected to each other, in the wheel (in this case, this wonderful flower) of life.

Cultural and Personal Differences: Discretion Is the Better Part of Disclosure

We have spoken throughout this book about honesty, and advocated for an unflinching examination of existential issues—of recognizing and working with death. We have nodded to other cultures and other ways of seeing this issue.

It is important to remember that the writers of this book are also influenced by their own cultural norms and expectations. Jerry is a physician and a scientist; that is in itself a culture. It deals in biological facts. It values disclosure and discourse about things that would be viewed as inappropriate in other contexts. Pam is a social worker of the "Let's all talk about *everything*" variety. Her viewpoints would be seen as rude and pushy by many others.

A physician friend of ours recently reminded us that many people do not feel comfortable discussing their deaths. Many people do not want to know what is at the end of the trail. They only want enough information to get through this week, this trial, this phase of the journey. These people are not in denial. There is nothing pathological or dysfunctional about their response to a life-threatening illness. It is consistent with the values and ethics of their culture, and it is supported by their friends and family.

For example, in many cultures, the anticipated death of either the matriarch or patriarch is not commonly discussed—if ever. These people have fixed and prominent positions within the family, and the position itself transcends the personalities of the individuals. In British public life, the passing of the queen is heralded by two simple sentences: "The queen is dead. God save the queen." In traditional Greek culture, the head of the family is so revered that it would be unthinkable to discuss his death before it occurred. When the patriarch dies, the next in line assumes that role immediately. There is no breach, but a continuance.

It is also important to remember that in many families, the role of the adult children is to protect, provide for, and make decisions on behalf of an elderly parent. In these families, the children may speak openly among themselves and may want to know all the medical information without disclosing this information to the dying parent. This is the way they nurture and show love and respect for their parents.

Whether you are a professional caregiver or a loving family member, in all circumstances, the best part of disclosure is discretion. Discretion is not secrecy. Discretion is the act of processing information with your head and with your heart and disclosing what you feel is consistent with the culture and personal beliefs of your family and which you believe is in best interests of your loved one.

Index

A

acetaminophen, 82
addiction, 80, 83
afterlife, 55, 89–90, 127
AIDS, 26–31, 37
analgesic, 80, 130–131
anesthesiologist, 80
anger, 57–59
"Annabel Lee," 101–102
antidepressants, 80, 84
anti-emetic, 80
anxiety management, 114–115
Apollinaire, Guillaume, 171
artwork therapy, 149–151, 173–174
aspirin, 82
assisted suicide, 123
authenticity, 97–100
authority, 107–108

B

bargaining, 62–63
Bartlow, Bruce, 139
bereavement support groups, 134
bodily functions, 118–119, 129–130
body
    changes in, 36–39
    death of, 127–129
    and self-image, 39, 40, 54
    and spirit, 22
brain death, 128
brain tumors, 46

breast cancer, 120–123
Browning, Elizabeth Barrett, 93
Buddhism, 127, 173
Buscaglia, Leo, 35

C

cancer
    brain tumors, 46
    breast, 120–122
    handling diagnosis of, 16–17
    and lymph system, 15–16
    receiving diagnosis of, 15–16
    responses to diagnosis of, 16–17
    stories of, 1–3, 75–76, 88–90, 104–107, 120, 142–143, 149–151, 166–168
    uterine, 15–17
carcinoma, 80
caregiving, 18, 22–24, 107–108, 120–122, 163, 165–168
Cassell, Eric, 52–56
chaplains, 68
chemotherapy, 80, 143
children
    death of, 137–146, 169–171
    and death of parent, 147–152
    grief of, 152
    memorializing, 146
    with special needs, 140
    talking about death, 151–152
    understanding of death, 147

Christianity, 112, 127
churches. *See* religion
colon cancer, 142
communication
    importance of, 50, 59–60
    listening, 19–20, 51
community, 6–8
compassion, 61, 132
contemplation, 18–20
control
    of death, 64–66
    need for, 44–47
convalescent hospitals, 118

D

death
    accepting, 100–107, 126
    acknowledgment of, 21, 103
    and anger, 57–59
    and authenticity, 97–100
    and bargaining, 62–63
    and breathing changes, 129
    and changes in roles, 176
    of children, 137–146, 169–171
    choosing location of, 65–66
    compensatory gains from, 47, 49–50
    contemplating, 18–20
    control of, 64–66
    cultural perceptions of, 127, 176
    and depression, 110–114
    and detachment from life, 110–114
    disclosing news of, 176
    discussion of, 176
    and dreams, 21–22
    effect on children, 147–148
    effect on family, 140–141

fears of, 14–17, 24, 46–47, 60, 99, 113–114, 170
fight against, 164
final tasks before, 91–94
and forgiveness, 91–92
and friendship, 25–31
and the future, 55
generational imperative of, 139–140
and good-byes, 94, 105–106, 132
and healing, 125–126
helplessness in, 114–116
at home, 117
and hope, 26–31, 55, 73–74, 110–114
in hospital, 70
letting go, 124
and life, 19
life after, 55, 89–90, 127
location of, 70, 117–118
and loneliness, 113
and loss of authority, 107–108
and love, 144–145
metaphors for, xviii–xix, 35–36, 110
moments after, 133–135
nature of, 20–21
paperwork for, 66–67
of parents, 147–152
perceptions of, 23, 127, 147, 176
personal nature of, 64
physician's role in, 163–171
physiologic aspect of, 127–129
preparation for, 32–34, 133
pronouncement of, 133
reflecting on, 49–56
and relationships, 86–90
representing effects of, 41–43

and resolution, 91–94
returning home for, 105–107
and sacredness, 12
social workers' help in, 68
spiritual perspective of, 21–22
stories of, 1–3, 4–5, 9–12, 26–31, 75–77, 88–90, 104–107, 120–122, 133, 142–143, 149–151, 166–168, 169–171
suspicion of, 14–17
and synchronicity, 9–12
talking to children about, 151–152
and thanksgiving, 92–93
and the unknown, 61
See also dying
depression, 84, 111–114
detachment, 111–114, 131
diagnosis
defined, 16
life after, 16–21
reception of, 15–16
responses to, 16–17
Dickinson, Emily, 63, 101, 111
disability insurance, 32
diseases
AIDS, 26–31, 37
cancer (*see* cancer)
diverticulitis, 38–39
emphysema, 40, 104
handling diagnosis of, 16–17
receiving diagnosis of, 16
treatment for, 164
diverticulitis, 38–39
"do not resuscitate" (DNR) status, 67
dreams, 21–22
drugs, 82–84

dying
and assisted suicide, 123
and authenticity, 99–100
from cancer, 1–3, 75–76, 88–90, 104–107, 120, 142–143, 149–151, 166–168
and changes in family roles, 17–18
and changes in social roles, 24–25, 119–122, 176
comfort while, 129–130
compensatory gains from, 47, 49–50
completing development through, 96–97
and dependence on others, 119–122
early stage of, 14–34
easing process of, 130–131
fear of, 14–17, 24, 46, 60, 99, 113, 170
feelings of loss in, 40–45
final stage of, 125–135
financial losses from, 31–32
getting help in, 116
and helplessness, 114–116
in hospitals, 71
and institutional care, 69–70
in isolation, 2–3
late stages of, 111–114
and life review, 49
losses during process of, 24–25
loss of authority from, 107–108
loss of bodily functions in, 118–119, 129–130
loss of control from, 41–47
and loss of safety, 40–43

maintaining balance through, 114–116

and medical equipment, 117

and memory, 51

metaphors for, xviii–xix, 14, 35–36, 73–74, 86, 110

and personal loss, 23–24

physical changes while, 36–39

preparation for, 32–34

process of, 20–21, 23–24

and self-esteem, 36–37, 39–40, 119–122

and self-examination, 100

sharing in process, 130–131

shock of, 18–19

stories of, 1–3, 4–5, 9–12, 26–31, 75–77, 88–90, 104–107, 120–122, 133, 142–143, 149–151, 166–168, 169–171

See also death

E

eating habits, 34

emergency pain pack, 131

emesis, 80

emotions, in dying, 50

emphysema, 40, 104

epidural, 80

exercise, 34

expenses, 31–32

F

"The Fall of Freddie the Leaf," 35

family

effect of death on, 17–18, 140–141

physical ties to, 54

fear

awareness of, 114

of death, 14–17, 24, 46–47, 60, 99, 113, 170

drugs for, 131

handling, 61, 113–114

managing, 114–116

sources of, 60

Field, Eugene, 137

Flanigan, Patrick, xvii, 48, 100

forgiveness, 91–92, 95–96

Frank, Anne, 125

friendships, 25–31. *See also* relationships

Frost, Robert, 2

funeral plans, 134–135

funerals, 135

future, 55

G

generational imperative, 139–143

Gibran, Kalil, 170

Gibson, W. W., 15

God

anger at, 59

bargaining with, 62–63

children's understanding of, 151–152

and death, 144–145

good-byes, 94, 105–106, 132

grief

of children, 147–151, 152

counseling for, 134, 140, 146, 152

cultural expression of, 57

from death of child, 138–146

expression of, 56–57

and guilt, 138

and isolation, xv
and loneliness, 57
manifestations of, 16–17
organizations for, 146
process of, 56–57
and religion, 140
Griffin, Jerry, xiii, 4–5
guilt
of caregivers, 165–168
over death of child, 138
effects of, 170
of physicians, 165–168, 170

H

health-care policies, 66–67
health-care professionals, 64
health insurance, 31–32
health maintenance organizations (HMOs), 31
heart attacks, 45, 104
helplessness, 114–116
home care, 26–27, 31, 116. *See also* hospice care
homosexuality, 26
hope, 26–31, 55, 73–74, 110–114
hospice care
advantages of, 64–66, 116
"do not resuscitate" (DNR) status, 67
effects of, 64–65
and grief counseling, 134
and health-care policies, 66–67
people involved in, 67–68
story of, 27–28
hospice houses, 118
hospice waiver, 66–67
hospital beds, 117
hospitals, 70–72, 118

Hyde, Carrie, xix, 23, 49

I

ibuprofen, 82
independence, loss of, 119–123
infusion, 80
In-Home Supportive Services (IHSS), 17
institutional care, 69–70
isolation, 59–62

J

Joeckel, Dieter, 125
Judaism, 112, 144–145
Jung, Carl, 7

L

life
and death, 19
detachment from, 111–114, 131
developmental tasks of, 96–97
metaphors for, xviii–xix, 14, 35–36, 73–74, 86, 110
and physical change, 36–39
prolonging, 124
reflecting on, 49–56
secrets of, 55
life review
and the afterlife, 55–56
and authenticity, 97–100
and behavioral changes, 54
cause of, 49–50
concepts of, 50–51
of family relationships, 53
and future concerns, 55
through memories, 52–53
through past illnesses, 53

and reconciliation, 91–94
of relationships, 53–54
of secrets, 55
self-concept in, 54
sharing in, 51–52
listening
importance of, 19–20, 51
tips for, 20
loneliness
dealing with, 113
preventing, 57, 134–135
story about, 75–76
love, expressing, 93
lung cancer, 166–168
lymphoma, 80
lymph system, 15–16

M

McLean, Don, 110
Medicaid, 31, 32
medical equipment, 117
medical expenses, 31–32
Medicare, 31, 32
medicine
antidepressants, 84
definitions in, 80
emergency pain pack, 131
limits of, 164
over-the-counter, 82
side effects of, 84
for stomach discomfort, 82–84
tolerance of, 83–84
meditation, 94–96
melanoma, 80
memorial services, 135
memories
endurance of, 55–56
in life review, 51–53

sharing, 130
"Mending Wall," 2
metastasis, 80
Millay, Edna St. Vincent, 58, 103, 112
Miller, Joaquin, 40
morphine, 83, 131
mortality, 164

N

narcotics, 80, 83
neoplasms, 80
nerve block, 80
nonsteroidal anti-inflammatory drugs (NSAIDS), 82
nurses, 67–68
nursing homes, 69–70, 118
nutrition, 34

O

Oliver, Sam, 6
over-the-counter drugs, 82

P

pain
and assisted suicide, 123
control of, 64–65
fear of, 123
managing, 78–79
medications for, 82
versus suffering, 65
paperwork, 66–67
parents
death of, 147–152
and death of children, 137–146, 169–171
PCA pump, 80

personal development, 96–97
pharmacology, 80
physical therapists, 68
physicians
    control of, 164–168
    limits of, 164
    relationship to patient, 163–171
physiologic death, 127–129
Poe, Edgar Allen, 101–102
poems
    "Annabel Lee," 101–102
    by Carrie Hyde, xix, 23, 49
    by Don McLean, 110
    by Dylan Thomas, 57
    by Edgar Allen Poe, 101–102
    by Edna St. Vincent Millay, 58, 103, 112
    by Elizabeth Barrett Browning, 93
    by Emily Dickinson, 63, 101, 111
    by Eugene Field, 137
    "The Fall of Freddie the Leaf," 35
    by Guillaume Apollinaire, 171
    by Helen Reddy, 147
    by Joaquin Miller, 40
    by Kalil Gibran, 170
    by Leo Buscaglia, 35
    by Margery Williams, 26, 97
    "Mending Wall," 2
    by Patrick W. Flanigan, xvii, 48, 100
    by Rainer Maria Rilke, 13, 60
    by Robert Frost, 2
    "Sorrow," 112
    "Spring," 58
    "Surviving the Storm," xvii, 100
    by Walt Whitman, 127
    "Well Worn," 48
    "What the Dying Teach Us," 6
    by W. W. Gibson, 15
post-traumatic stress disorder, 45
prayer, 33
preferred provider organizations (PPOs), 31
prescription drugs, 82

R

reconciliation, 91–96
Reddy, Helen, 147
reflection, 49–56
relationships
    authenticity in, 99–100
    changes in, 86–90
    loss of, 105–106
    between physician and patient, 163–171
    reconciliation in, 91–94
    review of, 53–54
religion
    Buddhism, 127, 173
    Christianity, 112, 127
    and grief, 140
    and illness, 17
    Judaism, 112, 144–145
    and suffering, 112–113
residential-care facilities, 69–70, 118
resolution, 91–96
respiration, 127
respite care, 118
Rilke, Rainer Maria, 13, 60–61

S

sadness, 113, 147–151
secret life, 55
self-concept, 51–54

self-esteem, 36–37, 39–40, 119–122
self-image, 36–40
Shakespeare, William, 56
social workers, 68
"Sorrow," 112
souls, 55
spiritual identity, 21–22
spirituality, 33
"Spring," 58
staging, 80
state disability program (SDI), 32
state of mind, 54
St. Vincent Millay, Edna, 58, 103, 112
sublingual, 80
suffering
    control of, 65
    dealing with, 112–114
    expression of, 59–60
    handling, 50–56
    importance of, 112–113
    versus pain, 64–65
    sharing in, 60–63
suicide, 123
"Surviving the Storm," xvii, 100
synchronicity, 6–12, 140–141

T

Tao Te Ching, 5
therapists, 68
therapy, through artwork, 149–151, 173–174
thanksgiving, 92–93
Thanksgiving Day, 73
Thomas, Dylan, 57
transcendence, 55–56
trust, loss of, 41–44
Tylenol, 82

U

Umann, Pam, xiii–xiv, 1–3
unknown, the, 61
uterine cancer, 15–17

V

volunteers, 68

W

"Well Worn," 48
"What the Dying Teach Us," 6
Whitman, Walt, 127
Williams, Margery, 26, 97

978-0-595-34426-0
0-595-34426-7